THE PENGUIN CLASSICS

FOUNDER EDITOR (1944–64): E. V. RIEU

FRANÇOIS-MARIE AROUET (1694–1778), who later took the name of VOLTAIRE, was the son of a notary and educated at a Jesuit school in Paris. His father wanted him to study the law, but the young man was determined on a literary career. He gained an introduction to the intellectual life of Paris, and soon won a reputation as a writer of satires and odes – a not altogether enviable reputation, for the suspicion of having written a satire on the Regent procured him a term of six months' imprisonment in the Bastille. On his release, his first tragedy, *Œdipe*, was performed (1718) in Paris with great success; and soon after he published the poem he had written in prison, a national epic, *La Henriade* (1724), which placed him with Homer and Virgil in the eyes of his contemporaries. After a second term of imprisonment in the Bastille, Voltaire spent three years (1726–9) in England, and returned to France full of enthusiasm for the intellectual activity and the more tolerant form of government he found in this country. His enthusiasm and his indictment of the French system of government are expressed in his *Philosophic Letters* (1733), whose sale was absolutely forbidden in France. The next fifteen years were spent at the country seat of his friend, Madame du Châtelet, where he wrote his most popular tragedies, and his *Zadig*, a witty Eastern tale, and started work on his *Century of Louis XIV*. After Mme. du Châtelet's death in 1749, Voltaire was induced to pay a prolonged visit to the Court of Frederick the Great, with whom he had been in correspondence for several years. While there he completed his important historical work *Essay on Customs* (*Essai sur les Mœurs et l'Esprit des Nations*), and began his *Philosophic Dictionary*. Voltaire and Frederick could not agree for long, and in 1753 Voltaire decided to leave Prussia. But he was not safe in France. After two years of wandering, he settled near Geneva, and at last made a home at Ferney. It was during these last, and most brilliant, twenty years of his life that he wrote *Candide*, his dialogues, and more tales, and published his widely-read *Philosophic Dictionary* (1764) in 'pocket' form, while conducting his ceaseless and energetic attack against what he called the 'infamous thing' — that is to say, all manifestations of tyranny and persecution by a privileged orthodoxy in Church and State. He died at the age of eighty-four, after a triumphant visit to the Paris from which he had been exiled for so long.

VOLTAIRE

CANDIDE

OR OPTIMISM

TRANSLATED BY
JOHN BUTT

PENGUIN BOOKS

Penguin Books Ltd, Harmondsworth, Middlesex, England
Penguin Books, 40 West 23rd Street, New York, New York 10010, U.S.A.
Penguin Books Australia Ltd, Ringwood, Victoria, Australia
Penguin Books Canada Ltd, 2801 John Street, Markham, Ontario, Canada L3R 1B4
Penguin Books (N.Z.) Ltd, 182–190 Wairau Road, Auckland 10, New Zealand

—

This translation first published 1947
Reprinted 1951, 1952, 1953, 1954, 1956 (twice), 1957, 1958, 1959, 1960,
1962, 1963, 1964, 1965, 1966, 1967, 1968 (twice), 1970 (twice),
1971, 1972, 1974 (twice), 1975, 1976, 1977, 1978, 1979 (twice), 1980,
1981, 1982 (twice), 1983, 1984

—

—

Made and printed in Great Britain
by Richard Clay (The Chaucer Press) Ltd,
Bungay, Suffolk
Set in Monotype Bembo

CONTENTS

CANDIDE OR OPTIMISM

CONTENTS

INTRODUCTION

VOLTAIRE was the wittiest writer in an age of great wits, and *Candide* is his wittiest novel. The subject he chose to exercise his wit upon in this novel is one which concerns all of us; surprisingly enough, that subject is the problem of suffering. However much we may try to avoid the problem, we are all confronted at some time with this difficulty, that the Creator has made a universe where suffering abounds. If the Creator is good and all-powerful, as we are told he is, could he not have made a better world? If he could, what prevented him? If he could not, can we still believe that he is good and all-powerful? Can we indeed believe in him at all? Or if we do, can we believe that he is at all concerned with men and their sufferings? In times of widespread disasters such questioning becomes more general and more urgent. We are living in such times; and so was Voltaire. When he wrote *Candide* in 1758 he was sixty-four years old, and had gained an immense reputation throughout Europe as a tragic dramatist, an epic poet, and a historian of a liberal cast of mind. He was living a life of strenuous retirement near Geneva, safe from the attacks of Church and State in France, whose enmity he had provoked by satire, lampoon, and ridicule directed against their authoritarian rule. He had known what personal suffering meant, for he had been imprisoned in the Bastille on suspicion of having lampooned the Regent, had been cudgelled at the orders of a courtier he had offended, and had been exiled from Paris; his study of history had convinced him that there is no such thing as Providence directing human affairs; and he had meditated on the calamities which had recently overtaken two large cities. In 1746 the greater part of Lima had been destroyed in an earthquake, and nine years later an even more catastrophic earthquake killed fifty thousand people in Lisbon. These disasters seemed a brutal comment on the current 'optimistic' philosophy of the day, a philosophy associated with the names of Leibniz, Shaftesbury, and Christian Wolff, and popularised both in France and England by Pope's *Essay on Man*. Philosophers like Candide's tutor, Dr. Pangloss, were maintaining that we live in the best of all possible worlds, where everything is connected and arranged for the best. What we regard as evil will, if rightly considered, be found conducive to the good of some other creature, and therefore necessary to the general design: we must put up with it, as best we can, for the sake of the general good. This doctrine is a perversion of Leibniz's teaching, and perhaps Voltaire knew it. At any rate, he made no attempt to meet the traditional Christian argument, reinterpreted by Leibniz, that evil cannot be excluded from a world in which we are free to choose evil or good, and that such a world is better than one where there would be no free agents, and therefore no evil and no good. With that argument he shows no concern. Though he ridiculed Leibniz's terminology, the *sufficient reason*, the *pre-established harmony*, and the *moral and physical evil* which were bandied about by Leibniz's disciples, he attacked, not Leibniz's philosophy, but its popular perversions.

Leibniz's doctrine, and the Christian doctrine he reinterprets, that a man's soul is tested in the freedom to choose evil or good and is perfected by suffering, are both liable to perversion. They must be expressed with the utmost tact. Both are 'optimistic': they explain the world in such a way as to give cause for hope—hope that the Creator is good, that he has created a good world, and that if only we could transcend the limitations of our humanity we should see that it is good. But the perversions of Leibniz current in Voltaire's time were pessimistic, since they offered only a counsel of despair to all but those who profited by the sufferings of their fellow-creatures: Pangloss and his kind excluded all hope. Even the Christian doctrine of purification by suffering can be made to sound callous by a preacher who does not know what suffering means; a tactful preacher will often need to exclaim, like the author of a popular modern exposition of this problem, 'How can I say with sufficient tenderness what here needs to be said?' It was the hopelessness and callousness of this perverted 'optimism' which angered Voltaire. His compassion for the victims of the earthquake and his sense of the impertinence and inadequacy of the 'Optimists'' comments were feelingly expressed in his *Poem on the Disaster of Lisbon* (1756). Some philosophers, he remarks in the preface to that poem, had explained to the people of Lisbon that all was for the best. 'The heirs of the dead would now come into their fortunes, masons would grow rich in rebuilding the city, beasts would grow fat on corpses buried in the ruins; such is the natural effect of natural causes. So don't worry about your own particular evil; you are contributing to the general good.' If anything could match the horror of the earthquake, it would be the cruelty of such a speech. That is Voltaire's comment; and he declares that if *All is for the best* is explained in an absolute sense, without offering hope for the future, it is only an insult added to the miseries we endure.

The callousness of the Optimists and the value of that eternal spring of hope are found once again in *Candide*, published in 1759, three years after the poem on Lisbon. But this time Voltaire was in a different mood. He is now Macaulay's Prince of Buffoons. 'He gambols; he grins; he shakes his sides; he points the finger; he turns up the nose; he shoots out the tongue.' But while the reader watches this display of merriment, he can never long forget that the buffoon is the same man who had cried, 'O God! Reveal to us that we must be human and tolerant.' Pangloss represents the disciples of Leibniz, repeating the master's terms but perverting his philosophy. Like the philosophers in Voltaire's preface to his poem, he is callous to Candide's injuries in the Lisbon earthquake and consoles the other sufferers with the assurance that things could not be otherwise. But Voltaire improved upon the mere conception of a Job's comforter—Pangloss is equally ready to expound the 'necessity' of his own sufferings, and to demonstrate the chain of events connecting the loss of his nose with Columbus's discovery of America. Even after he has been hanged at an auto-da-fé, dissected, and flogged at the bench of a Turkish galley, he is still faithful to his system, as absurdly sure as ever that he is living in the best of all possible worlds.

It is not only Pangloss who is made to suffer. The tortures, humiliations, and reversals of fortune which Candide and his friends undergo can all be traced in Voltaire's experience and reading—and could all be paralleled in these last few years of the world's history. In themselves they are not wildly absurd, and they become so only because no human being could endure all that Candide and his friends endure and live to tell the tale. But their number and variety serve Voltaire's purpose. He uses every device at his command to prevent our pity and to emphasise the resilience of human nature. In spite of all they suffer, they never despair, or not for long. The experiences of the old woman who attends Lady Cunégonde were more varied than the others could boast; but even she had met no more than twelve people who had voluntarily put an end to their miseries. Ridiculous as it seemed to her, she was still in love with life, in spite of everything she had been through. And that was true of the rest. Even Martin, who comes as near as any character to speaking with Voltaire's voice, is resigned rather than dejected, and takes a cynical pleasure in bursting bubble after bubble of hope as it springs in Candide's breast. For it is hope that buoys Candide through all his troubles. The hope of marrying the lovely Cunégonde takes him to South America; when he has lost her, the hope of finding her once more takes him through incredible and side-splitting adventures back again; and though he is disappointed when they ultimately meet, he can still hope for future happiness. That is Voltaire's answer to the 'Optimists'' counsel of despair.

The search for Cunégonde is one form which the search for happiness takes. This was a favourite theme with eighteenth-century writers, as readers of Dr. Johnson will remember, and Voltaire presents several variations on it. Like Swift in *Gulliver's Travels*, Voltaire takes his representative of mankind to that Paradise of eighteenth-century philosophers, the imaginary State conducted on principles of pure Reason. Swift placed it on an undiscovered island in the South Atlantic; Voltaire, who had been reading about the Incas in Garcilaso Inca de la Vega's *History of Peru*, located it on a plateau in the Andes surrounded by unscalable mountains. The details lifted from Garcilaso are sometimes grotesque; nevertheless Candide here finds all that the eighteenth-century Man of Reason could desire—a society in which all physical requirements are supplied, and where no one needs to go to law; where men have simplified religious belief to the lowest common denominator of natural religion; where neither crime nor war exist; where the achievements of science are respected; and where men enjoy equality and fraternity. This was certainly the best of all possible worlds, and Candide immediately recognised it; but he is unhappy in Paradise because the lovely Cunégonde is not there, and so his search continues. In the course of his travels with Martin he discovers the deception underlying the glitter of Parisian society, the misery which the prostitute's wantonness conceals, and the frustration of a monk's life in spite of its apparent prosperity. He pays a visit to a noble Venetian, who has all that money can buy and yet disdains it all. 'You must admit,' says Candide to Martin, 'that there is the happiest man alive, because he is superior to all he possesses'; but Candide admits, when pressed, that it is an empty life where nothing gives pleasure.

An empty life is the last danger that Candide has to face. He has lost most of his money, Cunégonde proves disappointing, and there is nothing to do but take part in everlasting metaphysical discussions with Pangloss. In this situation two chance visits teach him the principal lessons which Voltaire has to convey. A Turkish philosopher shows him the uselessness of metaphysical speculation, and a Turkish farmer the value of work. Candide goes home with the resolution to silence Pangloss and set his friends to a profitable exercise of their talents. The new scheme meets with Martin's entire approval: 'Let us work without arguing,' he says, in words very similar to those used by Voltaire at the end of the preface to his Lisbon poem; 'that's the only way to make life bearable.'

Such a survey does no justice to the wit and grace of Voltaire's story-telling, and to the amazing powers of invention he displays. These can be left to speak for themselves; and a translator may reflect that however difficult it is to recapture the grace of the original, he has only himself to blame if he fails to convey the wit; for Voltaire's wit is like the King of Eldorado's, dependent more upon the thought than the turn of phrase. The difficulty of conveying the grace of the original arises from a difference of economy and rhythm between French and English. A Frenchman usually needs fewer words than an Englishman to convey his meaning, and Voltaire increased the gap between the two languages by his sparse use of linking conjunctions and of the explanatory interjections in dialogue which we feel are needed to identify the speakers. A faithfully literal rendering of the French would often offend an English ear by its very baldness, and it has therefore been found necessary to expand the French in such places. Voltaire's economy in ligatures has an important effect on his rhythm. It allows him to vary the number of clauses and sentences which could be linked together in a rhythmical period. A literal rendering would sound harsh, and a translator must therefore abandon something of Voltaire's rhythm in the effort to make him speak modern English. For that is the ideal of translation. A translator should be able to say, as Dryden said of his version of Juvenal, 'I have endeavoured to make him speak that kind of English, which he would have spoken had he lived in England, and had written to this age.'

There is one more point to make. *Candide* has lost little of its general appeal. It still has ample power to entertain and to teach. But Voltaire wrote it for his contemporaries, who would all be familiar with the thought, the customs described, and the historical events referred to. While the modern reader will find nothing so obscure as to obstruct his enjoyment of the story, he may often wonder, even while he is laughing, just what event Voltaire had in mind, what details are true and what imaginary, and what a Manichean or a Jansenist believed. It is beyond the scope of this book to anticipate all that a reader might question. An attempt has been made, here and there, to paraphrase or insert a brief explanation into the course of the story where this could be tactfully and economically managed; but there are still a few questions which an English reader will probably want answered. He will at least want to know that the Bulgars and the Abars were two Scythian tribes of whom Voltaire had been reading in Pufendorf's *Introduction to the General and Political History of the Universe*, and whose names he chose to denominate the Prussians and the French; that Voltaire had met at Potsdam a gentleman who had been pressed for the Prussian army and treated exactly as Candide is treated in Chapter II; and that the Jesuits had established several little 'kingdoms' in

Paraguay within the Spanish dominions, where the natives worked for their spiritual overlords without material profit, as Cacambo infers (p. 62): in 1750 the Jesuits had resisted the transference of part of their territory from Spain to Portugal, and were defeated, only after several engagements, by the combined Spanish and Portuguese forces. The beggar from Artois mentioned on p. 108, whose attempt upon the life of Louis XV in 1757 had caused wholesale arrests, was Robert-François Damiens. His escapade recalled to the little *abbé's* mind the events of December 1594 rather than those of May 1610, because Damiens, like Jean Châtel in 1594, had failed to assassinate the King, whereas in 1610 François Ravaillac had succeeded. The English admiral whose execution Candide is made to witness (p.110) was Admiral John Byng, who was sentenced by court martial to death for failing to prevent the French from taking Minorca. Byng was shot at Portsmouth on March 14th, 1757, rather less than two years before *Candide* was written. The six strangers with whom Candide and Martin take supper (p. 124) were historical figures, and had all been deprived of their kingdoms. They were not all alive in 1759, however, Sultan Achmet having died in 1736, and Theodore of Corsica in 1756. Finally, the reader who is prompted to ask whether Pococurante's taste in books was shared by Voltaire can be assured that Voltaire had already expressed similar views about Homer, Virgil, Milton, Ariosto, and Tasso in his *Essay on Epic Poetry*. The curious reader may turn to M. André Morize's critical edition (1913), the text of which has been followed, without omissions, in this translation. The spurious second part is not included.

August 1946   J. B.

CANDIDE
OR OPTIMISM

Translated from the German
by Doctor Ralph

CHAPTER I

How Candide was brought up in a beautiful country house, and how he was driven away

THERE lived in Westphalia, at the country seat of Baron Thunder-ten-tronckh, a young lad blessed by nature with the most agreeable manners. You could read his character in his face. He combined sound judgment with unaffected simplicity; and that, I suppose, was why he was called Candide. The old family servants suspected that he was the son of the Baron's sister by a worthy gentleman of that neighbourhood, whom the young lady would never agree to marry because he could only claim seventy-one quarterings, the rest of his family tree having suffered from the ravages of time.

The Baron was one of the most influential noblemen in Westphalia, for his house had a door and several windows and his hall was actually draped with tapestry. Every dog in the courtyard was pressed into service when he went hunting, and his grooms acted as whips. The village curate was his private chaplain. They all called him Your Lordship, and laughed at his jokes.

The Baroness, whose weight of about twenty-five stone made her a person of great importance, entertained with a dignity which won her still more respect. Her daughter, Cunégonde, was a buxom girl of seventeen with a fresh, rosy complexion; altogether seductive. The Baron's son was in every way worthy of his father. His tutor, Pangloss, was the recognised authority in the household on all matters of learning, and young Candide listened to his teaching with that unhesitating faith which marked his age and character.

Pangloss taught metaphysico-theologo-cosmolo-nigology. He proved incontestably that there is no effect without a cause, and that in this best of all possible worlds, his lordship's country seat was the most beautiful of mansions and her ladyship the best of all possible ladyships.

'It is proved,' he used to say, 'that things cannot be other than they are, for since everything was made for a purpose, it follows that everything is made for the best purpose. Observe: our noses were made to carry spectacles, so we have spectacles. Legs were clearly intended for breeches, and we wear them. Stones were meant for carving and for building houses, and that is why my lord has a most beautiful house; for the greatest baron in Westphalia ought to have the noblest residence. And since pigs were made to be eaten, we eat pork all the year round. It follows that those who maintain that all is right talk nonsense; they ought to say that all is for the best.'

Candide listened attentively, and with implicit belief; for he found Lady Cunégonde extremely beautiful, though he never had the courage to tell her so. He decided that the height of good fortune was to have been born Baron Thunder-ten-Tronckh and after that to be Lady Cunégonde. The next was to see her every day, and failing that to listen to his master Pangloss, the greatest philosopher in Westphalia, and consequently the greatest in all the world.

One day Cunégonde was walking near the house in a little coppice, called 'the park', when she saw Dr. Pangloss behind some bushes giving a lesson in experimental physics to her mother's waiting-woman, a pretty little brunette who seemed eminently teachable. Since Lady Cunégonde took a great interest in science, she watched the experiments being repeated with breathless fascination. She saw clearly the Doctor's 'sufficient reason', and took note of cause and effect. Then, in a disturbed and thoughtful state of mind, she returned home filled with a desire for learning, and fancied that she could reason equally well with young Candide and he with her.

On her way home she met Candide, and blushed. Candide blushed too. Her voice was choked with emotion as she greeted him, and Candide spoke to her without knowing what he said. The following day, as they were leaving the dinner table, Cunégonde and Candide happened to meet behind a screen. Cunégonde dropped her handkerchief, and Candide picked it up. She quite innocently took his hand, he as innocently kissed hers with singular grace and ardour. Their lips met, their eyes flashed, their knees trembled, and their hands would not keep still. Baron Thunder-ten-tronckh, happening to pass the screen at that moment, noticed both cause and effect, and drove Candide from the house with powerful kicks on the backside. Cunégonde fainted, and on recovering her senses was boxed on the ears by the Baroness. Thus consternation reigned in the most beautiful and delightful of all possible mansions.

CHAPTER II

What happened to Candide amongst the Bulgars

AFTER being turned out of this earthly paradise, Candide wandered off without thinking which way he was going. As he plodded along he wept, glancing sometimes towards heaven, but more often in the direction of the most beautiful of houses, which contained the loveliest of barons' daughters. He lay down for the night in the furrow of a ploughed field with snow falling in thick flakes; and, to make matters worse, he had nothing to eat. Next day, perished with cold and hunger, and without a penny in his pocket, he dragged his weary limbs to a neighbouring town called Waldberghoff-trarbk-dikdorff, where he stopped at an inn and cast a pathetic glance towards the door.

Two men in blue noticed him.

'There's a well-made young fellow, chum,' said one to the other, 'and just the height we want.'

They went up to Candide and politely asked him to dine with them.

'Gentlemen,' said Candide modestly, 'I deeply appreciate the honour, but I haven't enough money to pay my share.'

'People of your appearance and merit, Sir, never pay anything,' said one of the men in blue; 'aren't you five feet five inches tall?'

'Yes, gentlemen, that is my height,' said Candide, with a bow.

'Very well, Sir, sit down; we'll pay your share, and what's more we shall not allow a man like you to go short of money. That's what men are for, to help each other.'

'You are quite right,' said Candide; 'for that is what Mr. Pangloss used to tell me. I am convinced by your courteous behaviour that all is for the best.'

His new companions then asked him to accept a few shillings. Candide took them gratefully and wanted to give a receipt; but his offer was brushed aside, and they all sat down to table.

'Are you not a devoted admirer . . .?' began one of the men in blue.

'Indeed I am,' said Candide earnestly, 'I am a devoted admirer of Lady Cunégonde.'

'No doubt,' replied the man; 'but what we want to know is whether you are a devoted admirer of the King of the Bulgars.'

'Good Heavens, no!' said Candide; 'I've never seen him.'

'Oh, but he is the most amiable of kings and we must drink his health.'

'By all means, gentlemen,' replied Candide, and emptied his glass.

'That's enough,' they cried. 'You are now his support and defender, and a Bulgar hero into the bargain. Your fortune is made. Go where glory waits you.'

And with that they clapped him into irons and hauled him off to the barracks. There he was taught 'right turn', 'left turn', and 'quick march', 'slope arms' and 'order arms', how to aim and how to fire, and was given thirty strokes of the 'cat'. Next day his performance on parade was a little better, and he was given only twenty strokes. The following day he received a mere ten and was thought a prodigy by his comrades.

The bewildered Candide was still rather in the dark about his heroism. One fine spring morning he took it into his head to decamp and walked straight off, thinking it a privilege common to man and beast to use his legs when he wanted. But he had not gone six miles before he was caught, bound, and thrown into a dungeon by four other six-foot heroes. At the court martial he was graciously permitted to choose between being flogged thirty-six times by the whole regiment or having twelve bullets in his brain. It was useless to declare his belief in Free Will and say he wanted neither; he had to make his choice. So, exercising that divine gift called Liberty, he decided to run the gauntlet thirty-six times, and survived two floggings. The regiment being two thousand strong, he received four thousand strokes, which exposed every nerve and muscle from the nape of his neck to his backside. The course had been set for the third heat, but Candide could endure no more and begged them to do him the kindness of beheading him instead. The favour was granted, his eyes were bandaged, and he was made to kneel down. The King of the Bulgars passed by at that moment and asked what crime the culprit had committed. Since the King was a man of great insight, he recognised from what he was told about Candide that here was a young philosopher utterly ignorant of the way of the world, and granted him a pardon, an exercise of mercy which will be praised in every newspaper and in every age. Candide was cured in three weeks by a worthy surgeon with ointments originally prescribed by Dioscorides; and he had just enough skin on his feet to walk, when the King of the Bulgars joined battle with the King of the Abars.

CHAPTER III

How Candide escaped from the Bulgars, and what happened to him afterwards

THOSE who have never seen two well-trained armies drawn up for battle, can have no idea of the beauty and brilliance of the display. Bugles, fifes, oboes, drums, and salvoes of artillery produced such a harmony as Hell itself could not rival. The opening barrage destroyed about six thousand men on each side. Rifle-fire which followed rid this best of worlds of about nine or ten thousand villains who infested its surface. Finally, the bayonet provided 'sufficient reason' for the death of several thousand more. The total casualties amounted to about thirty thousand. Candide trembled like a philosopher, and hid himself as best he could during this heroic butchery.

When all was over and the rival kings were celebrating their victory with Te Deums in their respective camps, Candide decided to find somewhere else to pursue his reasoning into cause and effect. He picked his way over piles of dead and dying, and reached a neighbouring village on the Abar side of the border. It was now no more than a smoking ruin, for the Bulgars had burned it to the ground in accordance with the terms of international law. Old men, crippled with wounds, watched helplessly the death-throes of their butchered women-folk, who still clasped their children to their bloodstained breasts. Girls who had satisfied the appetites of several heroes lay disembowelled in their last agonies. Others, whose bodies were badly scorched, begged to be put out of their misery. Whichever way he looked, the ground was strewn with the legs, arms, and brains of dead villagers.

Candide made off as quickly as he could to another village. This was in Bulgar territory, and had been treated in the same way by Abar heroes. Candide walked through the ruins over heaps of writhing bodies and at last left the theatre of war behind him. He had some food in his knap-sack, and his thoughts still ran upon Lady Cunégonde. His provisions were exhausted by the time he reached Holland, but as he had heard that everyone in that country was rich and all were Christians, he had no doubt that he would be treated as kindly as he had been at Castle Thunder-ten-tronckh before Lady Cunégonde's amorous glances caused his banishment.

He appealed for alms from several important-looking people, who all told him that if he persisted in begging he would be sent to a reformatory to be taught how to earn his daily bread.

At last he approached a man who had just been address-ing a big audience for a whole hour on the subject of charity. The orator peered at him, and said:

'What is your business here? Do you support the Good Old Cause?'

'There is no effect without a cause,' replied Candide modestly. 'All things are necessarily connected and arranged for the best. It was my fate to be driven from Lady Cunégonde's presence and made to run the gauntlet, and now I have to beg my bread until I can earn it. Things could not have happened otherwise.'

'Do you believe that the Pope is Antichrist, my friend?' said the minister.

'I have never heard anyone say so,' replied Candide; 'but whether he is or he isn't, I want some food.'

'You don't deserve to eat,' said the other. 'Be off with you, you villain, you wretch! Don't come near me again or you'll suffer for it.'

The minister's wife looked out of the window at that moment, and seeing a man who was not sure that the Pope was Antichrist, emptied over his head a pot full of . . . , which shows to what lengths ladies are driven by religious zeal.

A man who had never been christened, a worthy Anabaptist called James, had seen the cruel and humiliating treatment of his brother man, a creature without wings but with two legs and a soul; he brought him home and washed him, gave him some bread and beer and a couple of florins, and even offered to apprentice him to his business of manufacturing those Persian silks that are made in Holland. Candide almost fell at his feet.

'My tutor, Pangloss, was quite right,' he exclaimed, 'when he told me that all is for the best in this world of ours, for your generosity moves me much more than the harshness of that gentleman in the black gown and his wife.'

While taking a walk the next day, Candide met a beggar covered with sores. His eyes were lifeless, the end of his nose had rotted away, his mouth was all askew and his teeth were black. His voice was sepulchral, and a violent cough tormented him, at every bout of which he spat out a tooth.

CHAPTER IV

How Candide met his old tutor, Dr. Pangloss, and what came of it

CANDIDE was moved more by compassion than by horror at the sight of this ghastly scarecrow, and gave him the two florins he had received from James, the honest Anabaptist. The apparition looked at him intently and, with tears starting to his eyes, fell on the young man's neck. Candide drew back in terror.

'Does this mean,' said one wretch to the other, 'that you don't recognise your dear Pangloss any more?'

'Pangloss!' cried Candide. 'Can this be my beloved master in such a shocking state? What misfortune has befallen you? What has driven you from the most lovely of mansions? What has happened to Lady Cunégonde, that pearl among women, the masterpiece of nature?'

'My breath fails me,' murmured Pangloss.

At this Candide quickly led him to the Anabaptist's stable, where he made him eat some bread, and as soon as he had revived, said to him:

'You mentioned Cunégonde?'

'She is dead,' replied the other.

At these words Candide fainted, but his friend restored him to his senses with a little sour vinegar which happened to be in the stable. Candide opened his eyes.

'Cunégonde is dead!' said he. 'Oh, what has become of the best of worlds? . . . But what did she die of? No doubt it was grief at seeing me sent flying from her father's lovely mansion at the point of a jack-boot?'

'No,' said Pangloss. 'She was disembowelled by Bulgar soldiers after being ravished as much as a poor woman could bear. When my lord tried to defend her, they broke his head. Her ladyship was cut into small pieces, and my poor pupil treated in precisely the same way as his sister. As for the house, not one stone was left standing on another; not a barn was left, not a sheep, not a duck, not a tree. But we have been amply avenged, for the Abars did just the same in a neighbouring estate which belonged to a Bulgar nobleman.'

At this tale Candide fainted once more. When he recovered his senses, he first said all that was called for, and then enquired into cause and effect, and into the 'sufficient reason' that had reduced Pangloss to such a pitiable state.

'I fear it is love,' said his companion; 'love, the comforter of humanity, the preserver of the universe, the soul of all living beings; tender love!'

'I know what this love is,' said Candide, with a shake of his head, 'this sovereign of hearts and quintessence of our souls: my entire reward has been a kiss and twenty kicks on the backside. But how could such a beautiful cause produce so hideous an effect upon you?'

'My dear Candide,' replied Pangloss, 'you remember Paquette, that pretty girl who used to wait on our noble lady. In her arms I tasted the delights of Paradise, and they produced these hellish torments by which you see me devoured. She was infected, and now perhaps she is dead. Paquette was given this present by a learned Franciscan, who had traced it back to its source. He had had it from an old countess, who had had it from a cavalry officer, who was indebted for it to a marchioness. She took it from her page, and he had received it from a Jesuit who, while still a novice, had had it in direct line from one of the companions of Christopher Columbus. As for me, I shall not give it to anyone, for I am a dying man.'

'What a strange genealogy, Pangloss!' exclaimed Candide. 'Isn't the devil at the root of it?'

'Certainly not,' replied the great man. 'It is indispensable in this best of worlds. It is a necessary ingredient. For if Columbus, when visiting the West Indies, had not caught this disease, which poisons the source of generation, which frequently even hinders generation, and is clearly opposed to the great end of Nature, we should have neither chocolate nor cochineal. We see, too, that to this very day the disease, like religious controversy, is peculiar to us Europeans. The Turks, the Indians, the Persians, the Chinese, the Siamese, the Japanese as yet have no knowledge of it; but there is a 'sufficient reason' for their experiencing it in turn in the course of a few centuries. Meanwhile, it has made remarkable progress amongst us, and most of all in these huge armies of honest, well-trained mercenaries, who decide the destinies of nations. It can safely be said that when thirty thousand men are ranged against an army of equal numbers, there will be about twenty thousand infected with pox on each side.'

'I could listen to you for ever,' said Candide; 'but you must be cured.'

'How can I be cured?' said Pangloss. 'I haven't a penny, my dear friend, and there is not a doctor in all this wide world who will bleed you or purge you without a fee.'

This last remark decided Candide. He hurried to James, the charitable Anabaptist, and, falling at his feet, painted so moving a picture of the state to which his friend had been reduced that the good man did not hesitate to take Dr. Pangloss in and had him cured at his own expense. During treatment, Pangloss lost only an eye and an ear. He still wrote well and had a perfect command of arithmetic, so the Anabaptist appointed him his accountant. Two months later he was obliged to go to Lisbon on business and set sail in his own ship, taking the two philosophers with him. On the voyage Pangloss explained to him how all was designed for the best. James did not share this view.

'Men,' he said, 'must have somewhat altered the course of nature; for they were not born wolves, yet they have become wolves. God did not give them twenty-four-pounders or bayonets, yet they have made themselves bayonets and guns to destroy each other. In the same category I place not only bankruptcies, but the law which carries off the bankrupts' effects, so as to defraud their creditors.'

'More examples of the indispensable!' remarked the one-eyed doctor. 'Private misfortunes contribute to the general good, so that the more private misfortunes there are, the more we find that all is well.'

While he was pursuing his argument the sky became overcast, the winds blew from the four corners of the earth, and the ship was caught in a most terrible storm in sight of the port of Lisbon.

CHAPTER V

Describing tempest, shipwreck, and earthquake, and what happened to Dr. Pangloss, Candide, and James, the Anabaptist

HALF the passengers were at the last gasp of nervous and physical exhaustion from the pitching and tossing of the vessel, and were so weak that they had no strength left to realise their danger. The other half uttered cries of alarm and said their prayers, for the sails were torn, the masts were broken, and the ship was splitting. Work as they might, all were at sixes and sevens, for there was no one to take command. The Anabaptist gave what help he could in directing the ship's course, and was on the poop when a madly excited sailor struck him a violent blow, which laid him at full length on the deck. The force of his blow upset the sailor's own balance, and he fell head first overboard; but, in falling, he was caught on a piece of the broken mast and hung dangling over the ship's side. The worthy James ran to his assistance and helped him to climb on board again. The efforts he made were so strenuous, however, that he was pitched into the sea in full view of the sailor, who left him to perish without taking the slightest notice. Candide was in time to see his benefactor reappear above the surface for one moment before being swallowed up for ever. He wanted to throw himself into the sea after the Anabaptist, but the great philosopher, Pangloss, stopped him by proving that Lisbon harbour was made on purpose for this Anabaptist to drown there. Whilst he was proving this from first principles, the ship split in two and all perished except Pangloss, Candide, and the brutal sailor who had been the means of drowning the honest Anabaptist. The villain swam successfully to shore; and Pangloss and Candide, clinging to a plank, were washed up after him.

When they had recovered a little of their strength, they set off towards Lisbon, hoping they had just enough money in their pockets to avoid starvation after escaping the storm.

Scarcely had they reached the town, and were still mourning their benefactor's death, when they felt the earth tremble beneath them. The sea boiled up in the harbour and broke the ships which lay at anchor. Whirlwinds of flame and ashes covered the streets and squares. Houses came crashing down. Roofs toppled on to their foundations, and the foundations crumbled. Thirty thousand men, women and children were crushed to death under the ruins.

The sailor chuckled:

'There'll be something worth picking up here,' he remarked with an oath.

'What can be the "sufficient reason" for this phenomenon?' said Pangloss.

'The Day of Judgment has come,' cried Candide.

The sailor rushed straight into the midst of the debris and risked his life searching for money. Having found some, he ran off with it to get drunk; and after sleeping off the effects of the wine, he bought the favours of the first girl of easy virtue he met amongst the ruined houses with the dead and dying all around. Pangloss pulled him by the sleeve and said:

'This will never do, my friend; you are not obeying the universal rule of Reason; you have misjudged the occasion.'

'Bloody hell,' replied the other. 'I am a sailor and was born in Batavia. I have had to trample on the crucifix four times in various trips I've been to Japan. I'm not the man for your Universal Reason!'

Candide had been wounded by splinters of flying masonry and lay helpless in the road, covered with rubble.

'For Heaven's sake,' he cried to Pangloss, 'fetch me some wine and oil! I am dying.'

'This earthquake is nothing new,' replied Pangloss; 'the town of Lima in America experienced the same shocks last year. The same causes produce the same effects. There is certainly a vein of sulphur running under the earth from Lima to Lisbon.'

'Nothing is more likely,' said Candide; 'but oil and wine, for pity's sake!'

'Likely!' exclaimed the philosopher. 'I maintain it's proved!'

Candide lost consciousness, and Pangloss brought him a little water from a fountain close by.

The following day, while creeping amongst the ruins, they found something to eat and recruited their strength. They then set to work with the rest to relieve those inhabitants who had escaped death. Some of the citizens whom they had helped gave them as good a dinner as could be managed after such a disaster. The meal was certainly a sad affair, and the guests wept as they ate; but

Pangloss consoled them with the assurance that things could not be otherwise:

'For all this,' said he, 'is a manifestation of the rightness of things, since if there is a volcano at Lisbon it could not be anywhere else. For it is impossible for things not to be where they are, because everything is for the best.'

A little man in black, an officer of the Inquisition, who was sitting beside Pangloss, turned to him and politely said:

'It appears, Sir, that you do not believe in original sin; for if all is for the best, there can be no such thing as the fall of Man and eternal punishment.'

'I most humbly beg your Excellency's pardon,' replied Pangloss, still more politely, 'but I must point out that the fall of Man and eternal punishment enter, of Necessity, into the scheme of the best of all possible worlds.'

'Then you don't believe in Free Will, Sir?' said the officer.

'Your Excellency must excuse me,' said Pangloss; 'Free Will is consistent with Absolute Necessity, for it was ordained that we should be free. For the Will that is Determined . . .'

Pangloss was in the middle of his sentence when the officer nodded to his henchman, who was pouring him out a glass of port wine.

CHAPTER VI

How a magnificent auto-da-fé was staged to pre-
vent further earthquakes, and how Candide was
flogged

THE University of Coimbra had pronounced that the sight
of a few people ceremoniously burned alive before a slow
fire was an infallible prescription for preventing earth-
quakes; so when the earthquake had subsided after destroy-
ing three-quarters of Lisbon, the authorities of that country
could find no surer means of avoiding total ruin than by
giving the people a magnificent auto-da-fé.

They therefore seized a Basque, convicted of marrying
his godmother, and two Portuguese Jews who had refused
to eat bacon with their chicken; and after dinner Dr.
Pangloss and his pupil, Candide, were arrested as well, one
for speaking and the other for listening with an air of
approval. Pangloss and Candide were led off separately
and closeted in exceedingly cool rooms, where they
suffered no inconvenience from the sun, and were brought
out a week later to be dressed in sacrificial cassocks and
paper mitres. The decorations on Candide's mitre and
cassock were penitential in character, inverted flames and
devils without tails or claws; but Pangloss's devils had tails
and claws, and his flames were upright. They were then
marched in procession, clothed in these robes, to hear a
moving sermon followed by beautiful music in counter-
point. Candide was flogged in time with the anthem;

the Basque and the two men who refused to eat bacon were burnt; and Pangloss was hanged, though that was not the usual practice on those occasions. The same day another earthquake occurred and caused tremendous havoc.

The terrified Candide stood weltering in blood and trembling with fear and confusion.

'If this is the best of all possible worlds,' he said to himself, 'what can the rest be like? Had it only been a matter of flogging, I should not have questioned it, for I have had that before from the Bulgars. But when it comes to my dear Pangloss being hanged—the greatest of philosophers—I must know the reason why. And was it part of the scheme of things that my dear Anabaptist (the best of men!) should be drowned in sight of land? And Lady Cunégonde, that pearl amongst women! Was it really necessary for her to be disembowelled?'

He had been preached at, flogged, absolved, and blessed, and was about to stagger away, when an old woman accosted him and said:

'Pull yourself together, young man, and follow me.'

CHAPTER VII

How an old woman took care of Candide, and how he found the lady he loved

To pull himself together was easier said than done, but Candide managed to follow the old woman to a hovel, where she gave him something to eat and drink and a pot

of ointment to rub himself with. She then showed him
to a decent bed with a suit of clothes laid out beside it.

'Make a good meal,' she said, 'and have something to
drink, and get a good night's rest, and may Our Lady of
Atocha, St. Anthony of Padua, and St. James of Com-
postella take care of you! I shall come back in the morning.'

Astonished as he was with what he had already seen and
suffered, Candide was even more surprised at the old
woman's kindness. He wanted to kiss her hand, but the
old woman stopped him, saying:

'It is not *my* hand you should kiss. I will come back
to-morrow. In the meanwhile, rub yourself with that oint-
ment, take some food, and have a good night's rest.'

In spite of his misfortunes, Candide made a hearty meal
and slept soundly. The next morning the old woman
brought him his breakfast and examined his back, which
she rubbed herself with another ointment. At midday she
brought him his dinner, and returned in the evening with
his supper. The day after she did exactly the same.

'Who are you?' Candide kept asking her, 'and what
makes you so kind to me? How am I to thank you for
what you have done?'

But the good old woman would not reply. She returned
in the evening, but this time she brought him no supper.

'Come with me,' she said, 'and don't speak a word.'

She took him by the arm and led him out of the town
for about a quarter of a mile till they came to a lonely
house which stood in its own grounds surrounded by a
moat. The old woman knocked at a side door, which was
immediately opened, and led Candide up a private staircase
into a richly decorated boudoir. She showed him to a

brocaded couch, and then left him, shutting the door behind her. Candide could scarcely believe that he was awake; his past life seemed like a nightmare and the present moment a happy dream.

The old woman soon came back supporting with some difficulty a veiled and bejewelled lady of majestic build, who trembled as she drew near.

'Pull the veil aside,' said the old woman to Candide.

The young man approached, and timidly lifted the veil. He had the surprise of his life, for to his astonished gaze it seemed that Lady Cunégonde stood before him. And so, in fact, she did. Candide's strength left him, and he fell at her feet unable to speak a word. Cunégonde, too, was equally affected, and sank on to the couch. The old woman took some rose-water and sprinkled it over them. This brought them to their senses and they began to speak. Broken words came first, then half-uttered questions and answers, followed by sighs, tears, and groans. Seeing them well on the way to recovery, the old woman left them to themselves, advising them to make as little noise as possible.

'Can this really be Cunégonde?' cried Candide. 'You are still alive, then? . . . To think that I should find you in Portugal! . . . So you weren't ravished or disembowelled, as the learned Pangloss assured me?'

'I was indeed,' said the lovely Cunégonde, 'but people don't always die of those mishaps.'

'And your father and mother? Were they killed?'

'It is only too true,' said Cunégonde, with tears in her eyes.

'And your brother?'

'He was killed as well.'

'Now tell me why you are in Portugal and how you knew that I was here, and how you managed to have me brought to this house.'

'I will tell you all about it,' replied the lady; 'but first you must let me know everything that has happened to you since that innocent kiss you gave me and those kicks you received.'

Her wish was a law to Candide; and though he felt much abashed, and his feeble voice trembled as he spoke, and though his injured spine still hurt him a little, he told her everything that had happened to him from the moment of their separation in the most innocent way imaginable. Cunégonde was deeply affected, and shed tears at the death of Pangloss and the worthy Anabaptist. When Candide had finished, she told him her story, as follows, and you can well imagine that Candide, who gazed at her the whole time in rapt attention, did not miss a single word.

CHAPTER VIII

Cunégonde's story

'ONE night when I was fast asleep in bed, the Bulgars (by grace of God) arrived at our lovely Thunder-ten-tronckh and slaughtered my parents. They cut my father's throat and my brother's, and made mincemeat of my mother. A great lout of a Bulgar, six foot tall, noticed that I had fainted at the sight of this butchery, and set about ravishing me. That was enough to bring me round. I recovered my senses and cried for help, struggling, biting, and scratching as hard as I could. I wanted to tear the fellow's eyes out. You see, I didn't appreciate that what was happening in my father's house was in no way unusual. The brute gave me a wound in my left thigh, and I still bear the scar.'

'Oh, how I should like to see it!' exclaimed Candide, innocently.

'You shall,' said Cunégonde; 'but first let me go on with my story.'

'By all means,' said Candide.

Cunégonde continued: 'A Bulgar captain came in. He noticed that I was bleeding and that the soldier made no attempt to move. This lack of respect for an officer so enraged the captain that he slew the brute across my body. He then had my wound dressed and took me to his quarters as a prisoner of war. I used to wash his shirts for him (he hadn't many) and cook his meals. There is no denying he thought me pretty as well as useful, and I admit that he was quite handsome himself. His skin was certainly both white and soft, but apart from that I can say little for him. He had not much intelligence and little understanding of philosophy: it was quite clear that he had not been brought up by Dr. Pangloss. At the end of three months he had no money left, and as he had grown tired of me he sold me to Don Issachar, a Jew with business connexions in Holland and Portugal, who had a weakness for women. This Jew was much attached to my person, but he could not get his way with me, for I was more successful in resisting him than the Bulgar soldier. A woman of honour can be ravished once, but the experience is a tonic for her virtue. To make me more amenable, the Jew brought me to this country house where we are sitting. I used to think,' she continued, as she looked round her boudoir, 'that there was no place so beautiful as Castle Thunder-ten-tronckh, but I see that I was wrong.

'One day the Grand Inquisitor noticed me at Mass. He ogled me persistently, and sent a message to say he had something to discuss with me in private; so I was brought to his palace. I told him of my birth, whereupon he showed me how I was degrading myself in belonging to an Israelite. A proposal was then made to Don Issachar that he should surrender me to His Eminence. Don Issachar, who is the Court banker, and therefore a man of some standing, would not hear of the proposition, until the Inquisitor threatened him with an auto-da-fé. This forced the Jew's hand, but he made a bargain by which this house and I should belong to both of them in common, to the Jew on Mondays, Wednesdays, and Sabbath days, and to the Inquisitor the other days of the week. This agreement has now lasted for six months. There has been some quarrelling, as they cannot decide whether Saturday night belongs to the old law or to the new. For my part I have resisted both of them so far, and I think that is why they love me still.

'In course of time His Eminence made up his mind to prevent the disaster of another earthquake, and to intimidate Don Issachar, by celebrating an auto-da-fé, to which he did me the honour of inviting me. I had an excellent seat, and delicious refreshments were served to the ladies between Mass and the execution. I confess I was horrified at seeing those two Jews burned, and that honest Basque who had married his godmother; but imagine my surprise, my fright and distress, at seeing a figure that looked like Pangloss, dressed in the sacrificial cassock and paper mitre! I rubbed my eyes and watched attentively till I saw him hanged. Then I fainted; but scarcely had I recovered my senses when my eyes lighted on you, standing there stark naked. You can fancy what horror and consternation, what grief and despair I felt. Your skin, I assure you, is much whiter than my Bulgar captain's; it has a much more delicate bloom. The sight roused feelings which overwhelmed and consumed me. I screamed, and wanted to shout: "Stop, you Barbarians!" But my voice failed me, and indeed my cries would have been useless. When you had been thoroughly flogged, I said to myself, "What can have brought my adorable Candide and our wise Pangloss to Lisbon, one to receive a hundred lashes and the other to be hanged at the orders of that same Cardinal Inquisitor who is so devoted to me? I am afraid Pangloss cruelly deceived me when he told me that all is for the best in this world."

'You can well imagine how distracted I was. One moment I was almost beside myself with frenzy, the next I was at death's door from very faintness. And all the time my mind kept recurring to my parents' butchery and my brother's slaughter, then to the insolence of that brutal Bulgar soldier and the wound he gave me, then to my slavery as a kitchen-maid and to my Bulgar captain, and that wretched Don Issachar and the hateful Inquisitor, then back to Dr. Pangloss's execution and the magnificent anthem in counterpoint performed while you were being flogged. But above all my mind dwelt on the kiss you gave me behind the screen that day when I saw you for the last time, and I praised God for bringing you back to me through so many trials. I ordered my old servant to take care of you and bring you here as soon as she could, and she has faithfully carried out my wishes. It gives me inexpressible pleasure to see you again and to listen to you and talk to you; but you must be ravenous. I am feeling famished myself. So let's have supper.'

They sat down to table together, and after supper reclined on the beautiful couch already mentioned. There they were when Don Issachar, one of the masters of the house, arrived. It being the Sabbath day, he had come to enjoy his rights and unfold the tenderness of his love.

CHAPTER IX

Relating further adventures of Cunégonde, Candide, the Grand Inquisitor, and the Jew

ISSACHAR was the most excitable Hebrew that had been seen in Israel since the Babylonian Captivity.

'So you are not satisfied with the Inquisitor, you Galilean bitch,' he shouted, 'but this rogue must be given a share as well?'

With these words he drew a long dagger, which he always carried, and hurled himself at Candide without pausing to think whether his opponent was armed. It so happened that the old woman had given our worthy Westphalian not only a suit of clothes but a beautiful sword, which he now drew and, gentle though his manners were, laid the Israelite out on the floor, dead as a door-nail, at the feet of the lovely Cunégonde.

'Holy Virgin!' she exclaimed. 'What will happen to us now? A man killed in my house! If the police come, we are done for.'

'If Pangloss had not been hanged,' said Candide, 'he would have given us good advice in this emergency, for he was a great philosopher. Failing him, let's consult the old woman.'

She was a person of remarkable discretion, and was just starting to give her opinion when another secret door opened. It was one hour after midnight, and therefore Sunday morning, a day which belonged to the Cardinal Inquisitor. He entered, and saw before him the man whom he had had flogged, with a sword in his hand, a dead body lying on the floor, Cunégonde frightened out of her wits, and the old woman offering advice.

Candide made up his mind in an instant. His reasoning was as follows:

'If this holy man calls for help, he will assuredly have me burnt, and Cunégonde, too, in all probability. I have been mercilessly whipped at his orders; besides, he's my rival. I've got into the way of killing people. There's no time to hesitate.'

His reflections were clear and rapid; and without giving the Inquisitor time to recover from his surprise, he ran him through and laid him beside the Israelite.

'Here's another scrape!' cried Cunégonde. 'There will be no mercy! We are excommunicated for certain! Our last hour has come! A gentle creature like you to kill a Jew and a priest in the space of two minutes! What could you have been thinking about?'

'Dearest lady,' replied Candide 'a jealous man in love

doesn't know what he is doing, especially if he has been whipped by the Inquisition.'

The old woman then resumed her advice, and said:

'There are three thoroughbreds in the stable, with saddles and bridles. The gallant Candide must get them ready. You, Madam, have some moidores and diamonds. We must make haste and ride to Cadiz, although I can hardly keep my seat with only one buttock. The weather could not be finer, and we shall enjoy travelling in the cool of the night.'

Candide immediately saddled the three horses, and Cunégonde, the old woman, and he covered thirty miles without baiting. They had scarcely made their escape when the police arrived at the house. The Cardinal was buried in a beautiful church, and Issachar was thrown on the dunghill.

In the meanwhile Candide, Cunégonde, and the old woman had reached the little town of Avacena in the Morenian hills, where we find them next engaged in conversation in an inn.

CHAPTER X

Describing the distressing circumstances in which Candide, Cunégonde, and the old woman reached Cadiz, and how they set sail for the New World

'WHO could have robbed me of my moidores and diamonds?' cried Cunégonde, bursting into tears. 'What are we to live on? Whatever shall we do? Where shall I find more Inquisitors and Jews to replace them?'

'I strongly suspect that reverend friar who slept at the same inn with us yesterday at Badajoz,' said the old woman, wringing her hands. 'I don't like jumping to a hasty conclusion, but I remember that he entered our room twice and left the inn long before we did.'

'Our excellent Pangloss often proved to me,' said Candide, with a sigh, 'that worldly goods are common to all men, and that everyone has an equal right to them. That being so, the friar certainly ought to have left us enough to finish our journey. Dearest Cunégonde, have you nothing left?'

'Not a farthing,' she replied.

'Then what are we to do?' said Candide.

'We must sell one of the horses,' said the old woman. 'I will ride behind my lady (though I can hardly keep my seat with only one buttock), and we will reach Cadiz somehow.'

A Benedictine prior, who was staying at the same inn, bought the horse from them for a few pesetas, and Candide, Cunégonde, and the old woman reached Cadiz at last by way of Lucena, Chillas, and Lebrija. At Cadiz a fleet was being victualled and some troops assembled for enforcing the claims of reason upon the Jesuits of Paraguay, who were accused of inciting one of their tribes near the town of St. Sacrament to rebel against the Kings of Spain and Portugal. Having served with the Bulgars, Candide was able to show his proficiency in Bulgar drill in front of the General of this little force, and made so favourable an impression by his grace and swiftness, his bearing, nimbleness, and valour, that he was appointed to command a company of infantry. Behold him now a captain, embarking with Lady Cuné-

gonde, the old woman, two man-servants, and the two
horses which had belonged to the Grand Inquisitor of
Portugal.

During the voyage they argued incessantly about poor
Pangloss's philosophy.

'We are going to a different world,' said Candide, 'and
I expect it is the one where all goes well; for I must admit
that regrettable things happen in this world of ours, moral
and physical acts that one cannot approve of.'

'I love you with all my heart,' said Cunégonde, 'but I
still shudder at the thought of what I have seen and
experienced.'

'Everything will turn out right,' replied Candide; 'why,
even the sea round this new world is better than our Euro-
pean seas; it is calmer, and the winds are less variable. It is un-
doubtedly the new world that is the best of all possible
universes.'

'God grant it may be!' said Cunégonde; 'but I have been
so terribly unfortunate in my affairs, that I have lost almost
all hope.'

'The way you both complain!' exclaimed the old woman.
'You haven't had misfortunes like mine to bear, I assure
you.'

Cunégonde started to titter with laughter, for it was
amusing of the good woman to pretend to be more un-
fortunate than she.

'My dear, good Abigail,' she said, with an emphatic shake
of her head, 'unless you have been ravished by two Bulgars,
had two stabs in your belly, and two of your country
houses demolished; unless you have had two mothers and
two fathers butchered before your eyes, and beheld two of

your lovers flogged at an auto-da-fé, I don't see how you can rival me, especially as I am a baron's daughter with seventy-two quarterings in my coat of arms, and yet have served as a kitchen-maid.'

'Madam,' replied the old woman, 'you know nothing of my birth; and if I were to show you my behind you you wouldn't talk as you do, but would suspend judgment.'

This speech excited the curiosity of Cunégonde and Candide, and the old woman continued in these words:

CHAPTER XI

The old woman's story

'My eyes were not always sore and bloodshot, my nose did not always touch my chin, and I have not always been a servant. I am the daughter of Pope Urban X and the Princess of Palestrina.* Until the age of fourteen I was brought up in a palace whose very stables were grander than all the mansions of your German barons, and any one of my dresses was worth more than all the magnificence of Westphalia. I daily increased in beauty, grace, and accomplishments, and was surrounded by delights of all kinds. I met with tokens of respect and excited expectations wherever I went; and I was already an object of desire. My breast grew shapely, and what a lovely breast it was! White as a lily, and as firmly and elegantly moulded as the Venus de

* Notice how exceedingly discreet our author is. There has so far been no Pope called Urban X. He hesitates to ascribe a bastard to an actual Pope. What discretion! What a tender conscience he shows! [*Voltaire's note.*]

Medici's. And when I think of my eyes and those marvellous eyelids and jet-black brows, I remember how our local poets used to tell me that the flames which burned so brightly in those two pupils of mine outshone the twinkling of the stars. The women who dressed and undressed me fell back in ecstasy as they looked at me before and behind; and there was not a man who did not yearn to change places with them.

'I was betrothed to a sovereign prince of Massa-Carrara, assuredly the very pattern of all princes. He was my equal in beauty, a paragon of grace and charm, sparkling with wit, and burning with love. I adored him to distraction, to the point of idolatry: I loved him as one can never love twice. The marriage was to be celebrated with unparalleled pomp and magnificence. It was a continual round of feasting, dancing, and carnival, and the whole of Italy was engaged in writing me sonnets, not one of which was worth reading. The highest point of my happiness was at hand when an old marchioness, who had been my Prince's mistress, invited him to drink chocolate with her. He died less than two hours later in horrible convulsions; but that is a mere trifle. My mother was less afflicted than I was by this blow, yet even her despondency was such that she decided to leave this melancholy scene for a while and visit a beautiful estate which she owned near Gaeta. We set sail in a yacht gilded as richly as the altar of St. Peter's at Rome, but had not gone far when a Moorish pirate bore down upon our ship and attacked us. Our soldiers defended themselves like the Pope's guard: they fell on their knees and threw away their arms, begging the pirates for absolution at the point of death.

'They were immediately stripped stark naked, and so were my mother, our ladies-in-waiting, and I. It is wonderful how quickly these gentlemen can strip people; but what surprised me more was that they put their fingers into a place where we women normally admit nothing but a syringe-tube. This seemed to me an unusual custom, but that is how we regard everything new when we first leave our native country. I soon discovered that they wanted to make sure we had not hidden any diamonds there, a practice dating from time immemorial among civilised seafaring nations. I learnt that the Maltese Knights of St. John never fail to observe it when they capture any Turks and their ladies; and it is, in fact, an established point of international law which has never been called in question.

'I need not tell you what a hardship it was for a young princess and her mother to be carried to Morocco as slaves, and you can readily imagine what we had to suffer on board the pirate ship. My mother was still a beautiful woman, and our ladies-in-waiting, even our chambermaids, had more charms than can be found in the whole of Africa. As for me, I was ravishingly lovely, the pattern of beauty and grace; and I was a virgin—but not for long. That flower of maidenhood, which had been reserved for the handsome Prince of Massa-Carrara, was torn from me by the pirate captain, an odious negro, who even fancied he was doing me an honour. The Princess of Palestrina and I must certainly have been mighty strong to withstand all we had to undergo before reaching Morocco. But that's enough: such experiences are so common that they are not worth the trouble of describing.

'Morocco was swimming in blood when we arrived.

The fifty sons of the Emperor Muley Ismael each had his faction, which in effect created fifty civil wars of blacks against blacks, blacks against tawnies, tawnies against tawnies, and mulattoes against mulattoes. It was perpetual massacre throughout the length and breadth of the empire.

'We had scarcely disembarked when some blacks of a hostile faction turned up to carry off my pirate's booty, of which we were the most precious part except for the gold and diamonds. I then witnessed a fight such as you would never see the like of in European climates. Northern races are not sufficiently warm-blooded; their lust for women does not reach the mania that is so common in Africa. It seems that Europeans have milk in their veins, but it's fire and vitriol that runs in the veins of those who live on Mount Atlas and round about. They fought like the lions, tigers, and serpents of their country to decide who should have us. A Moor seized my mother by the right arm, and my captain's lieutenant held her by the left; a Moroccan soldier took her by one leg, while one of our pirates clung to the other. Almost all our women were immediately disputed in the same fashion by four soldiers apiece. My captain kept me hidden behind him, and with his scimitar slew everyone who confronted him. In the end I saw my mother and all our Italian ladies torn limb from limb, slashed, and massacred by the monsters that fought for them. All were killed, both captors and captives, my companions, the soldiers, sailors, blacks, whites, and mulattoes, and finally my pirate chief; and I myself lay dying on a heap of corpses. Scenes such as these took place all over that country, as I know full well—and it is three hundred leagues across. Yet they will not miss one of the five daily prayers prescribed by Mahomet.

'I freed myself with considerable trouble from the pile of bleeding corpses, and managed to crawl to the shade of a large orange tree on the banks of a stream nearby. There I collapsed, exhausted and famished, overcome by fear, horror, and despair; and soon after I fell asleep, if I may so describe what was more like a trance than slumber. I was in this state of weakness and insensibility, hovering between life and death, when I felt myself pressed by something stirring on my body. I opened my eyes and beheld a good-looking man of fair complexion who sighed as he muttered: "*O che sciagura d'essere senza coglioni!*"

CHAPTER XII

The old woman's misfortunes continued

'ASTONISHED and delighted as I was to hear my native language, I was none the less surprised at the words the man uttered. I replied that there were greater misfortunes than what he complained of, and I had told him briefly the horrors I had experienced before I fell into another swoon. He carried me to a house nearby, where I was given something to eat and put to bed. He waited on me, comforted me, and caressed me, telling me that he had never seen anyone so beautiful nor had ever so keenly regretted what no one could restore to him.

' "I was born at Naples," he told me, "where they

castrate two or three thousand children every year. Some of them die, some acquire a more beautiful voice than any woman has, and others become Prime Ministers. My operation was a great success, and I became organist to the Princess of Palestrina."

' "To my mother!" I exclaimed.

' "Your mother?" he cried, with tears starting to his eyes. "Then you must be that young Princess I taught till she was six years old, who was promising even then to be as beautiful as you are now!"

' "You are quite right," I replied; "four hundred yards from here you will find my mother cut into four pieces and lying under a heap of corpses."

'I told him all that had happened to me, and he described his adventures as well. He told me how he had been sent to the King of Morocco by a Christian prince to make a treaty with that monarch for the supply of gunpowder, cannons, and warships to enable him to destroy the trade of other Christian Powers.

' "I have completed my mission," said the honest eunuch, "and am going to leave from Ceuta. I will take you back to Italy with me. *Ma che sciagura d'essere senza coglioni!*"

'I was touched by his kindness, and the tears started to my eyes as I thanked him. Instead of taking me to Italy, however, he brought me to Algiers and sold me to the Governor of that province. Scarcely had I been sold when the plague, which had spread through Africa, Asia, and Europe, broke out in Algiers with increased fury. You know what earthquakes are like, Madam; but have you ever had the plague?'

'Never,' replied Cunégonde.

'If you had,' replied the old woman, 'you would agree

that it is much worse than an earthquake. It is very common in Africa, and I caught it. Just imagine the situation of a Pope's daughter, fifteen years old, who in the space of three months had suffered poverty and slavery, had been ravished almost every day, seen her mother quartered, endured the horrors of famine and battle, and was then dying of plague in Algiers. I didn't die, however; but my eunuch did, and so did the Governor and almost the entire Algerian harem.

'When the first ravages of this terrible plague had subsided, the Governor's slaves were sold. A trader bought me and took me to Tunis. There he sold me to another trader, who took me to Tripoli and sold me once more. From Tripoli I was taken to Alexandria, from Alexandria to Smyrna, and from Smyrna to Constantinople. I changed hands at each place, and in the end found myself belonging to a captain of the Sultan's guard, who soon afterwards was ordered to the defence of Azov against the Russians.

'This captain, who was a most civil man, took the whole of his harem with him, and housed us in a small fortress on the Sea of Azov, where we were guarded by two black eunuchs and twenty soldiers. A vast number of Russians was killed, but they gave us as good as they got. Azov was burnt to the ground and the inhabitants were slaughtered without regard to age or sex. All that was left was our little fortress, which the enemy decided to starve out. The twenty soldiers who guarded us had sworn never to surrender; but the extremes of hunger to which they were reduced forced them to eat our two eunuchs for fear of breaking their oath. A few days later they decided to eat the women.

'We had a Mohammedan priest in our fortress, a most pious and compassionate man. He preached a beautiful sermon to the soldiers persuading them not to kill us outright. "Cut just one buttock off each of these ladies," he said, "and that will provide you with a delicious meal; if you find you need more, you can have as much again in a few days' time. Allah will be pleased at such a charitable action, and the siege will be relieved."

'His eloquence persuaded them, and we accordingly suffered this horrible operation. The priest anointed us with the same ointment that is used after children have been circumcised. I assure you we were all at death's door.

'Scarcely had the Turkish soldiers finished the meal we had supplied when the Russians arrived in flat boats: not one Turk escaped. The Russians paid no attention to the state we were in. But wherever you go, you find French surgeons; one of them, a very clever man, took care of us and cured us, and I shall never forget how he solicited me as soon as my wounds were completely healed. He also said what he could to console us, assuring us that similar things had happened at several sieges and that it was quite in accordance with the laws of warfare.

'As soon as my companions could walk, we were all sent to Moscow. I was knocked down at a sale to a Russian nobleman, who made me his gardener and whipped me twenty times a day. Two years later he was broken on the wheel with about thirty other noblemen for some intrigue at Court, so I seized the opportunity of escaping and made my way across Russia. For a long time I was a barmaid at an inn in Riga. From there I went to Rostock, then to Vismar, then to Leipzig, Cassel, Utrecht, Leyden, the

Hague, and Rotterdam. I have grown old (with only half a behind) in misery and shame, but I have never forgotten that I am the daughter of a Pope. I have wanted to kill myself a hundred times, but somehow I am still in love with life. This ridiculous weakness is perhaps one of our most melancholy propensities; for is there anything more stupid than to be eager to go on carrying a burden which one would gladly throw away, to loathe one's very being and yet to hold it fast, to fondle the snake that devours us until it has eaten our hearts away?

'In the countries where it has been my fate to wander and in the inns where I have worked I have met a vast number of people who detested their existence, but I have met only twelve who have voluntarily put an end to their misery—three negroes, four Englishmen, four Swiss, and a German professor called Robeck. I ended by being a servant in the house of Don Issachar, the Jew. He made me your waiting-woman, dearest lady, and I am now linked to your destiny and more concerned with your adventures than with my own. I should never even have spoken of my misfortunes if you had not provoked me a little, and if it were not the custom to pass the time on board ship by telling stories. So you see, Madam, that I am a woman of experience: I know the world. Just to amuse yourself, persuade each passenger to tell you his story, and if you find even one who has not often cursed his life and told himself that he is the most miserable man alive, you can throw me into the sea head first.'

CHAPTER XIII

How Candide was forced to leave the lovely Cunégonde and the old woman

HAVING heard the old woman's story, the lovely Cunégonde began to pay her all the respect due to a person of her rank and quality. She agreed to her proposal and persuaded all the passengers in turn to tell her their adventures. Candide and she had to admit that the old woman was right.

'It is a great pity,' said Candide, 'that the normal custom at an auto-da-fé was broken and our sagacious Pangloss hanged: for otherwise he would have made some remarkable observations on the moral and physical evils which infest the earth and sea, and with all due respect to him I should have made bold to offer a few objections.'

While each passenger was telling his story the ship was making good progress, and at last reached Buenos Ayres, where Cunégonde, Captain Candide, and the old woman landed and went to wait upon the Governor, Don Fernando d'Ibaraa y Figueora y Mascarenes y Lampourdos y Souza, a nobleman with a degree of pride appropriate to one who bore so many names. He spoke to people with lordly contempt and with his nose in the air, and he harangued so loudly and unsparingly, assuming so imposing an attitude, and affecting such an arrogant bearing that everyone who saluted him wanted to hit him. He had an ungovernable greed for women, and since Cunégonde appeared to him the most beautiful woman he had ever seen, the first thing he did was to ask if she were the captain's wife. The manner in which he put the question alarmed Candide. He did not dare to say she was his wife, because in fact she was not. He did not dare to say she was his sister, because that was not true either; and though the white lie was fashionable with the ancients and can be useful to the moderns, his soul was too pure to commit such treason against truth.

'Lady Cunégonde intends to do me the honour of being my wife,' he said, 'and we humbly entreat your Excellency to be so condescending as to attend our wedding.'

Don Fernando d'Ibaraa y Figueora y Mascarenes y Lampourdos y Souza smiled grimly; and giving a twirl to his moustaches, he ordered Captain Candide to go and review his troops. Candide obeyed, and the Governor was left alone with Lady Cunégonde. He declared his passion to her and swore that he would marry her the following day with the Church's blessing or without, just as a lady of such charming appearance should prefer. Cunégonde begged a quarter of an hour's grace to collect her thoughts, and went to take the old woman's advice on what to do.

'Madam,' said the old woman to Cunégonde, 'you have seventy-two quarterings to your coat of arms but not a farthing to your name; you have only yourself to blame if you do not become the wife of the greatest nobleman in South America with the most handsome of moustaches. What right have you to pride yourself on an unshakable fidelity? Remember that you have been ravished by the Bulgars, that a Jew and an Inquisitor have enjoyed your favours, and reflect that misfortunes bring some privileges.

I confess that, if I were in your place, I should have no hesitation in marrying the Governor and making the captain's fortune.'

While the old woman was speaking with the prudence which age and experience confer, a cutter was seen entering the harbour with a Spanish magistrate and officers of the secret police on board. This is what had happened:

The old woman had been quite right in thinking that it was a friar with long sleeves who had stolen Cunégonde's money and jewels at Badajoz, when she and Candide were making their escape to Cadiz. The friar tried to sell some of the stones to a jeweller, but the shopman recognised them as the property of the Grand Inquisitor. Before he was hanged the friar confessed that he had stolen them, and described the persons he had robbed and the direction they had taken. Cunégonde's flight with Candide was already known; they were followed to Cadiz, and no time was lost in sending a ship in pursuit. The ship was now in Buenos Ayres harbour, and the rumour soon spread that a Spanish magistrate was disembarking in pursuit of the murderers of the Grand Inquisitor. The prudent old woman immediately saw what was to be done.

'You cannot escape,' she told Cunégonde, 'but you have nothing to fear. It was not you who killed His Eminence; and besides, the Governor loves you so violently that he will not allow you to be molested. So stay where you are.'

She then hurried away to find Candide. 'Make haste and be off,' she cried, 'or you'll be burnt at the stake in an hour!'

There was no time to lose . . . but how was he to leave Cunégonde, and where was he to find shelter?

CHAPTER XIV

The reception Candide and Cacambo met with from the Jesuits of Paraguay

CANDIDE had brought from Cadiz the type of servant often found on the Spanish coasts as well as in the colonies. He was a quarter Spaniard of half-breed Argentine stock, and had been successively chorister, verger, sailor, monk, commercial traveller, soldier, and footman. His name was Cacambo, and he was devoted to his master because his master was a very good fellow. On hearing the old woman's news, he promptly saddled the two thoroughbreds, and said:

'Let's take her advice, Sir, and make off while the coast is clear.'

But Candide burst into tears.

'My darling Cunégonde,' he exclaimed, 'to have to leave you just when the Governor had promised to come to our wedding! What's to become of you, Cunégonde, now I have brought you so far from home?'

'She'll be all right,' said Cacambo. 'Women are never at a loss. God looks after them. . . . Hurry up, Sir.'

'Where are you taking me?' asked Candide. 'Where are we going? What shall we do without Cunégonde?'

'Why, surely!' said Cacambo. 'You were going to make war against the Jesuits. Let's go and fight on their side instead. I am pretty sure of the way, so I'll take you to their kingdom. They will be delighted to have a captain trained

in the Bulgar army, and you will make a vast fortune.
When you don't get what you expect on one side, you find
it on the other. Fresh sights and fresh adventures are always
welcome.'

'So you have already been to Paraguay?' said Candide.

'Indeed I have,' replied Cacambo. 'I was once a servant
in the College of the Assumption, so I know how the
reverend fathers govern as well as I know the streets of
Cadiz. It's a wonderful system they have. There are thirty
provinces in their kingdom, and it is more than three
hundred leagues across. The reverend fathers own the
whole lot, and the people own nothing: that's what I call a
masterpiece of reason and justice. I don't think I have ever
seen such godlike creatures as the reverend fathers. They
fight the Kings of Spain and Portugal over here and give
them absolution in Europe. In this country they kill
Spaniards, and in Madrid they send them to Heaven.
Delightful, isn't it? . . . But we must keep moving. You
will be the happiest man alive. How pleased the fathers
will be to have a captain trained in the Bulgar army!'

As soon as they reached the first frontier post, Cacambo
told the guard that a captain wanted to speak to his rever-
ence, the Colonel. A soldier was sent to inform Head-
quarters, while a Paraguayan hurried to the Colonel to
tell him the news. Candide and Cacambo were first of
all disarmed and deprived of their two horses. They
were then conducted between two ranks of soldiers to
the officer, who stood at the end of the row, halberd in
hand and sword at his side, with his biretta on his head
and his cassock tucked up. He made a sign, at which
twenty-four soldiers surrounded the two new-comers.

A sergeant told them that they must wait; the Colonel could not speak to them, he said, because his reverence, the Father Provincial, did not allow any Spaniard to open his mouth except in his presence, nor to stay more than three hours in the country.

'Where is his reverence, the Father Provincial?' asked Cacambo.

'He has said Mass, and now he has gone on parade,' replied the sergeant. 'You will not be able to kiss his spurs for another three hours.'

'But the Captain isn't a Spaniard,' said Cacambo. 'He's a German, and he is dying of hunger like me. Can't we have something to eat while we are waiting for his reverence?

The sergeant went straight off to report this conversation to the Colonel.

'Praise be to God,' said this dignitary, 'I can speak to him as he is a German. Have him brought to my arbour.'

Candide was immediately conducted to a nook amongst the trees, decorated with a pretty colonnade of green and gold marble and with lattice-work cages containing humming-birds, birds of paradise, parakeets, guinea-fowl, and other rare birds. An excellent dinner was served on gold plates, and while the Paraguayans ate their maize on wooden dishes in the open field in the full blaze of the sun, his reverence the Colonel retired to the shade of his arbour.

He was a handsome young man with a round face and fresh complexion. He had arched eyebrows and bright eyes; the tips of his ears were red and his lips scarlet. Though he looked proud, his arrogance was neither of the Spanish nor of the Jesuit kind. Candide and Cacambo were given back both their arms and their two horses, and

Cacambo had some oats brought to the arbour so that he could keep a sharp eye on the horses, for fear of a surprise.

Before sitting down to table, Candide kissed the hem of the Colonel's cassock.

'So you are a German,' began the Jesuit in that language.

'Yes, your reverence,' said Candide.

As they spoke, they looked at each other in astonishment, and seemed unable to control their emotion.

'What part of Germany do you come from?' asked the Jesuit.

'From that dirty province of Westphalia,' replied Candide. 'I was born at Castle Thunder-ten-tronckh.'

'Good gracious me!' exclaimed the Colonel. 'You don't mean to say so!'

'How extraordinary!' exclaimed Candide.

'Can this really be you?' said the Colonel.

'This is beyond the bounds of possibility!' said Candide.

They both fell back in amazement, and then embraced each other and burst into tears.

'Are you really the lovely Cunégonde's brother, your reverence?' said Candide. 'Why, you were killed by the Bulgars, weren't you? Are you sure you are the Baron's son? Fancy your being a Jesuit in Paraguay! This world is a strange place, I must confess. How happy our dear Pangloss would be if he had not been hanged!'

Some negro slaves and Paraguayans were pouring wine into glasses of rock crystal. The Colonel dismissed them, and folding Candide in his arms, gave thanks to God and St. Ignatius while the tears streamed down his face.

'You will be even more astonished,' said Candide, who was weeping as copiously as the Colonel, 'you will be even more excited and moved to hear that your sister, Lady Cunégonde, who, you thought, was disembowelled, is in the best of health.'

'Where is she?'

'Not far off; she's with the Governor of Buenos Ayres; and I had come to make war on you.'

Every word they spoke during this long conversation revealed some new marvel, and their eyes shone with the excitement of talking and listening. Since they were Germans, they continued to sit over their meal while waiting for the reverend Father Provincial; and the Colonel addressed his dear Candide in these words:

CHAPTER XV

How Candide killed the brother of his beloved Cunégonde

As long as I live I shall remember that terrible day when I saw my father and mother killed and my sister ravished. When the Bulgars withdrew, that darling sister was nowhere to be found, and my mother, my father, and I were thrown into a cart with two servants and three little boys who had been massacred, and were taken to be buried in a Jesuits' chapel two leagues from our family seat. A Jesuit sprinkled holy water on us. It was salt water, and a few drops of the disgusting stuff got into my eyes. The reverend father, noticing my eyelids flicker, put his hand to my heart and felt it beating; so I was rescued, and at the end of three weeks I had quite recovered. You know, my dear Candide, what a good-looking boy I was: well, I grew up more handsome still, and the reverend father Croust, the father superior of the house, took a fancy to me. He made me a novice; and shortly afterwards, I was sent to Rome because the Father General of the Society needed some young German Jesuit recruits. The rulers of Paraguay accept as few Spanish Jesuits as they can; they prefer strangers, since they think they can get the better of them. So I was selected by the reverend father general to go and work in this vineyard, and I set off with two others, a Pole and a Tyrolean. On arrival I was appointed subdeacon and lieutenant, and to-day, I am a colonel and a priest. We are engaging the King of Spain's troops with the utmost vigour, and I assure you they will be excommunicated and beaten. Surely Providence has sent you here to help us. But is it really true that my dear sister Cunégonde is in the neighbourhood, staying with the Governor of Buenos Ayres?'

Candide swore that it was absolutely true, and tears started to their eyes once more.

The Baron called Candide his brother and saviour, and embraced him times without number.

'My dear Candide,' he said, 'I feel sure that we shall ride in triumph through the town and rescue my sister, Cunégonde.'

'That's what I am longing for,' said Candide, 'because I was expecting to marry her; and indeed I still hope to.'

'You insolent fellow!' exclaimed the Baron. 'You have the impudence to think of marrying my sister, who has

seventy-two quarterings in her coat of arms, and you dare
to talk to me of such a hot-headed notion? Have you no
sense of shame?'

Candide was dumbfounded at this outburst:

'Reverend father,' he replied, 'all the quarterings in the
world would make no difference. I rescued your sister
from the arms of a Jew and of an Inquisitor. She is under
the deepest obligations to me, and she wants to be my wife.
My master Pangloss used to tell me that men are equal;
and I shall marry her without any hesitation.'

'We shall see about that, you rascal,' said the Jesuit Baron
von Thunder-ten-tronckh; and with those words he struck
him across the face with the flat of his sword.

Candide instantly drew his own and plunged it up to the
hilt in the Baron's stomach, but as he withdrew the dripping
blade he began to weep, and cried: 'O God! What have I
done! I have killed my old master, my friend, and my
brother-in-law! I am the best-tempered man there ever
was, yet I have already killed three men, and two of them
were priests!'

Cacambo, who had been standing sentinel at the arbour
door, rushed in.

'There is nothing left but to sell our lives dearly,' said
his master. 'They will undoubtedly break into the arbour,
and we must die sword in hand.'

Cacambo had often been in similar trouble, so he kept
his head. He took the Jesuit gown off the Baron and put it
on Candide, handed him the dead man's square hat and
made him mount his horse. It was all done in the twinkling
of an eye.

'Gallop, Sir,' cried Cacambo; 'everyone will take you

for a Jesuit with despatches to deliver, and we shall have crossed the frontier before they can run after us.'

With these words he rushed ahead, crying in Spanish: 'Make way, make way for the reverend father Colonel!'

CHAPTER XVI

The adventures of our two travellers with two girls and two monkeys, and what happened to them amongst the savage Oreillons

CANDIDE and his servant were over the frontier before anyone in the camp had discovered the German Jesuit's death. The provident Cacambo had taken care to fill his haversack with bread, chocolate, ham, fruit, and some bottles of wine; so they plunged ahead on their thorough-breds into an unknown country where there were no roads to be found. At last a beautiful meadow interlaced with streams came into view, where they decided to stop and refresh their horses. Cacambo suggested that his master should take something to eat and began to set him an example.

'How can you ask me to eat ham,' said Candide, 'when I have killed the Baron's son, and see myself condemned never to set eyes again on my lovely Cunégonde for the rest of my life? What is the use of prolonging my miserable existence, if I must drag out my days in remorse and despair at being banished from her presence? And what will the Jesuit periodicals say?'

While giving vent to these melancholy reflections he was making a hearty meal. Just as the sun was setting the two wanderers heard some faint cries which sounded like women's voices. They could not tell whether they were cries of grief or of joy, but they rose hurriedly with that sense of anxiety and alarm which everything arouses in an unknown country. They found that the cries came from two naked girls who were tripping along the edge of the meadow, while two monkeys followed them nibbling their buttocks. Candide's heart was touched by the sight. He had learnt how to shoot with the Bulgars and could have hit a nut on a bush without touching the leaves, so, taking up his double-barrelled Spanish rifle, he fired and killed the two monkeys.

'Thank Heaven for that, my dear Cacambo!' he exclaimed. 'I have delivered those two poor creatures from grave danger. If I sinned in killing an Inquisitor and a Jesuit, I have made ample amends in saving the lives of these two girls. I dare say they are young ladies of noble birth; and the adventure may therefore prove most useful to us in this country.'

He was about to continue in this vein, but stopped abruptly on seeing the two girls fondly embracing the two monkeys and shedding tears over their bodies, while they filled the air with most pitiful cries.

'I have never seen such magnanimity,' said he to Cacambo, after he had surveyed the scene for some time.

'A pretty piece of work, Sir!' said Cacambo. 'You have killed those two young ladies' lovers.'

'Their lovers? Impossible! You're laughing at me, Cacambo! I simply can't believe you.'

'My dear Master,' replied Cacambo, 'everything seems to surprise you. Why should you find it so strange that in some parts of the world monkeys obtain ladies' favours? They are partly human, just as I am partly Spanish.'

'I am afraid you must be right,' replied Candide, 'for I remember hearing Professor Pangloss say that similar accidents used to happen in the old days, and that such unions produced centaurs, fauns, and satyrs. He told me that several great men in ancient times had seen them. But I used to dismiss it all as mere fable.'

'Well, this ought to convince you that it is true,' said Cacambo; 'for you see how people behave who have not received a certain type of education. All I fear is that these ladies will play us some dirty trick.'

These solid reflections urged Candide to leave the meadow and take shelter in a wood. He and Cacambo sat down to supper, and after they had cursed the Inquisitor of Portugal, the Governor of Buenos Ayres, and the Baron, they both fell asleep on a mossy bank. When they awoke they discovered they could not move, the reason being that during the night they had been tied to a tree with ropes of pith by the Oreillons, the inhabitants of the country, to whom the two ladies had denounced them. They found themselves surrounded by some fifty naked Oreillons, armed with arrows, clubs, and stone axes: some of them were heating a large cauldron, while others were preparing skewers, and the whole mob was crying, 'He's a Jesuit! He's a Jesuit! We shall have our revenge and enjoy a good meal. We'll have Jesuit for dinner, we'll have Jesuit for dinner!'

'My dear Master,' cried Cacambo sadly, 'I told you those two girls would play us some dirty trick.'

'We shall certainly be roasted or boiled,' cried Candide, on noticing the cauldron and the skewers. 'What would Professor Pangloss say if he had seen how unsophisticated nature behaves? No doubt all is for the best, but I must say it is very cruel to have lost Lady Cunégonde and to be skewered by the Oreillons.'

Cacambo never lost his head. 'Don't despair,' he said to the dejected Candide; 'I know a little of their lingo, so I'm going to talk to these people.'

'Then don't fail to make them understand,' said Candide, 'how outrageously inhuman it is to cook their fellow-men, and that it's scarcely the act of a Christian.'

'So you reckon, gentlemen,' said Cacambo, 'that to-day you are going to eat a Jesuit? I have no objection; it is quite right to treat your enemies in that way. In fact, the laws of nature teach us to kill our fellow-creatures, and that is what happens in every corner of the earth. If we don't observe the custom of eating them, it is because we have other means of making a good meal. But you haven't the same resources as we have, and it is certainly much better to eat your enemies than to leave the fruits of victory to crows and ravens. But, gentlemen, you would not wish to eat your friends. You think you are going to skewer a Jesuit; but it's your defender, the enemy of your enemies, that you are about to roast. For my part, I was born in your country; and as for this gentleman, my master, he is so far from being a Jesuit that he has just killed one and carried off his spoils: that is how you came to be mistaken. To make sure that what I tell you is true, take his gown, carry it to the nearest frontier post of the fathers' kingdom, and find out if my master has not killed a Jesuit officer. You will not be losing much time, for you will still be able to eat us if you find that I have been lying to you. But if I have been telling you the truth, you are too well acquainted with the principles and customs of international law not to use us courteously.'

The Oreillons were impressed by Cacambo's reasoning, and commissioned two of their leaders to make post haste and find out the truth. The two delegates acquitted themselves intelligently and soon returned with good news. The Oreillons then released their two prisoners and treated them with every civility. They offered them girls, gave them refreshments, and led them back to the borders of their kingdom, merrily shouting: 'He was never a Jesuit! Not he!'

Candide was full of admiration and kept harping on his deliverance. 'What grand people they are!' he said. 'What fine fellows! And what culture! If I had not been lucky enough to spit Lady Cunégonde's brother, I should infallibly have been eaten. When all is said and done, there is a sterling goodness in unsophisticated Nature; for instead of eating me, these people behaved most politely as soon as they learnt that I was not a Jesuit.'

CHAPTER XVII

*How Candide and his servant reached the country of
Eldorado and what they saw there*

WHEN they reached the Oreillon frontier, Cacambo said to
Candide:

'The new world, you see, is no better than the old; take
my advice, and let's return to Europe as quickly as we can.'

'But how are we to get there?' said Candide. 'And
where are we to go when we arrive? If I go to my own
country, I shall find Bulgars and Abars cutting everybody's
throats; if I return to Portugal, I shall be burnt alive; and if
on the other hand we stay in this country, we run a con-
stant risk of being skewered. But, in any case, how can I
decide to leave that part of the world where Lady Cuné-
gonde is living?'

'Let us make for Cayenne,' said Cacambo. 'We shall
find some of those globe-trotting Frenchmen there, and
they will be able to help us. Perhaps God will have pity on
us in the end.'

It was not easy to get to Cayenne. They had a rough
idea which direction to take, but they found formidable
obstacles everywhere in the shape of mountains, rivers,
precipices, brigands, and savages. Their horses died from
fatigue, and their provisions were exhausted. For an entire
month they existed on wild fruits; but at last they reached
a stream whose banks were lined with coco-nut trees, which
helped to support life and keep their spirits up.

Cacambo, whose advice was as consistently good as the old woman's, said to Candide:

'We can't go any farther; we have walked far enough. I see an empty boat tied to the bank; let's fill it with coconuts, step on board, and drift downstream with the current. A river always leads to some inhabited place. If we don't find anything pleasant, we shall at least find something fresh.'

'Very well,' said Candide, 'we'll do as you suggest, and trust in Providence.'

The stream took them several miles between banks which at one point were smooth and covered with flowers, and at another were rocky and sterile. The river grew wider and wider, and at last disappeared into a cave under some cliffs of terrifying height, whose summits seemed to touch the sky. The two travellers were courageous enough to trust themselves to the stream as it rushed under the cliffs, while the river, narrowing once more, carried them on with frightening speed and noise. At the end of twenty-four hours they emerged into the light of day; but their boat was dashed to pieces against some boulders and they had to creep from rock to rock for three whole miles, until at length they reached a vast open plain, surrounded by inaccessible mountains. The farmer and the landscape gardener had been equally busy in this countryside, and everything which served the needs of man was pleasing to the sight. The roads were crowded, or rather adorned, with carriages, magnificent in appearance and material, drawn by huge red sheep faster than the finest horses of Andalusia, Tetuan, or Mequinez, and in them sat men and women of matchless beauty.

'This is a better sort of country than Westphalia,' said

Candide, while he and Cacambo were making for the nearest village.

As they approached they noticed some children, covered with tattered gold brocade, playing at ninepins; and our two visitors from the other world stopped to watch them. Their skittles were large round objects of striking brilliance, some of them yellow, some red, and some green. The travellers had the curiosity to pick some up, and found that they were gold nuggets, emeralds, and rubies, the least of which would have been the grandest ornament in the Mogul throne.

'These children playing at ninepins,' said Cacambo, 'are no doubt the sons of the King of this country.'

At that moment the village schoolmaster appeared to send the children back to school.

'That must be the tutor to the Royal Family,' said Candide.

The little urchins stopped playing, and left their skittles and other toys in the road. Candide picked them up and, running after the tutor, handed them to him with a deep bow and made signs to show that Their Royal Highnesses had forgotten their gold nuggets and precious stones. The village schoolmaster smiled and threw them away, surveying Candide for a moment with great surprise before continuing his walk.

The travellers did not fail to pick up the gold, emeralds, and rubies.

'Where can we have got to?' cried Candide. 'The children of the Kings of this country must be well brought up, if they are taught to despise gold and precious stones.' And Cacambo was as surprised as Candide.

In due course they approached the largest house in the village, which looked like a European palace. A crowd of people was standing round the door, and there were more inside. Strains of delightful music could be heard, and a delicious smell of cooking reached them. Cacambo went up to the door, and heard Peruvian spoken. It was his mother tongue, for you will remember that Cacambo was born in an Argentine village where that was the only language they knew.

'I will be your interpreter,' said he to Candide. 'Let's go inside. This is an inn.'

Two waiters and two waitresses, dressed in cloth of gold with their hair tied in ribbons, invited them to sit down to table and put before them four tureens of soup, each garnished with two parakeets, a boiled vulture weighing about two hundred pounds, two delicious roast monkeys, three hundred doves on one plate, and six hundred humming-birds on another, as well as exquisite stews and luscious pastries, all served on plates of a sort of rock crystal. And the waiters and waitresses offered them several kinds of liqueurs to drink made from sugar cane.

The guests were tradesmen and waggoners for the most part and were all extremely polite. They put several questions to Cacambo with delicate tact, and answered the enquiries he made to his complete satisfaction.

When the meal was over, Cacambo thought—as indeed did Candide—that two of the large gold nuggets they had picked up would amply pay their bill, but when they placed them on the table the landlord and his wife laughed so long and so loud that they had to hold their sides. They recovered their composure at last, and the landlord said:

'Gentlemen, it is obvious that you are strangers here, and we are not used to foreigners. So please excuse our laughter at your offering to pay us with stones off the road. I dare say you haven't any of our money, but you don't need any to dine here. All inns run for the convenience of tradespeople are paid for by the Government. You have fared badly here because this is a poor village, but everywhere else you will be received as you deserve to be.'

Cacambo interpreted the landlord's remarks to Candide, and Candide heard them with the same wonder and bewilderment that his friend Cacambo showed in translating them.

'What country can this be?' said one to the other. 'It must be unknown to the rest of the world, because everything is so different from what we are used to. It is probably the country where all goes well; for there must obviously be some such place. And whatever Professor Pangloss might say, I often noticed that all went badly in Westphalia.'

CHAPTER XVIII

What they saw in the country of Eldorado

CACAMBO tried to satisfy his curiosity by questioning the landlord, but all the landlord would say was: 'I am an ignorant fellow and quite content to be so. But we have an old man in the neighbourhood who has retired from Court; he is the most learned person in the kingdom, and he will certainly be able to satisfy you.' So he took Cacambo to call on the old man, while Candide played a minor part and accompanied his valet. They walked over to a modest little house, and went in. The door was mere silver, and the rooms were panelled with nothing better than gold; but the workmanship was in such good taste as to vie with the richest panelling. It is true that the hall was incrusted only with rubies and emeralds, but everything was so well designed as to compensate for this extreme simplicity.

The old man was seated on a couch stuffed with humming-bird feathers when the two strangers were shown in. He begged them to sit down, and offered them liqueurs in diamond glasses. After this refreshment he began to satisfy their curiosity as follows:—

'I am one hundred and seventy-two years old,' he said. 'It was from my late father, who was equerry to the King, that I learned about the astonishing Peruvian revolution of which he was an eye-witness. The kingdom where we live used to be inhabited by the Incas, who imprudently left it to subdue another part of the world, and were finally exterminated by the Spaniards.

'A few noblemen had been wise enough to stay behind in their native country. With the agreement of the whole nation, they made a law that no inhabitant should ever leave our little kingdom; and that is how our innocence and happiness have been preserved. The Spaniards had a confused knowledge of the existence of this country, which they named Eldorado, and an English nobleman called Ralegh nearly reached it about a hundred years ago; but as we are surrounded by unscalable rocks and precipices, we have so far been sheltered from the greed of European nations, who have a quite irrational lust for the pebbles and dirt found in our soil, and would kill every man of us to get hold of them.'

Their conversation was a long one and covered the form of government in Eldorado, local customs, behaviour towards women, public ceremonies, and the arts. At last Candide, whose taste for metaphysics was insatiable, told Cacambo to ask whether any religion was practised in the country.

The old man blushed slightly. 'Religion!' he exclaimed. 'Why, of course there's a religion. Do you suppose we are lost to all sense of gratitude?'

Cacambo humbly asked him what the religion of Eldorado was. The old man blushed once more.

'Can there be two religions, then?' said he. 'I have always believed that we hold the religion of all mankind. We worship God from morning till night.'

'Do you worship only one God?' asked Cacambo, interpreting Candide's doubts.

'Of course we do,' said the old man. 'There is only one God, not two, three, or four. What odd questions you foreigners ask!'

Candide was indefatigable in plying the good old man with questions. He wanted to know how prayers were offered to God in Eldorado.

'We never pray,' said this good and venerable man; 'we have nothing to ask of God, since He has given us everything we need. But we thank Him unceasingly.'

Candide was curious to see some of their priests, and told Cacambo to ask where they could be found.

The old man smiled. 'My friends,' said he, 'we are all priests; the King and the heads of each family perform solemn hymns of thanksgiving every morning, with an orchestra of five or six thousand musicians to accompany them.'

'Do you mean to say you have no monks teaching and disputing, governing and intriguing, and having people burned if they don't subscribe to their opinions?'

'We should be stupid if we had,' said the old man; 'we are all of the same opinion here, and we don't know what you mean by monks.'

Candide was delighted with all he heard, and said to himself: 'This is quite different from Westphalia and the Baron's mansion: if our friend Pangloss had seen Eldorado, he would not have kept on saying that Castle Thunder-ten-tronckh was the loveliest house on earth; it shows that people ought to travel.'

When this long conversation was over, the good old man had a carriage and six sheep made ready, and commissioned twelve of his servants to take the two travellers to Court.

'I must beg you,' said he, 'to excuse me from accompanying you; my great age deprives me of that honour. You will have no reason, I am sure, to be discontented with your reception from the King; but if any of the customs of this country should happen to displease, no doubt you will make allowances.'

Candide and Cacambo took their seats in the carriage, and the six sheep made such speed that in less than four hours they reached the King's palace, which stood at one end of the capital. The portico was two hundred feet high and one hundred broad, but it is impossible to describe what it was made of. Nevertheless, the prodigious superiority of its materials over the sand and pebbles which we call gold and precious stones was clearly manifest.

Twenty maidservants of surpassing beauty welcomed Candide and Cacambo as they alighted from their carriage, and led them to a dressing-room, where they fitted them out with garments of humming-bird down. Dressed in these robes of State, they were conducted by lords and ladies of the Court to wait upon His Majesty, and passed through an antechamber, on each side of which two ranks of a thousand musicians had been placed, in accordance with the normal custom. As they approached the throne room, Cacambo asked one of the lords-in-waiting how he should behave in saluting His Majesty; should he fall on his knees or should he grovel, should he put his hands on his head or his behind, or should he lick the dust off the floor; in short, what was the procedure?

'The custom is,' said the lord-in-waiting, 'to embrace the King and kiss him on both cheeks.'

Accordingly, Candide and Cacambo fell on His Majesty's neck, and were most graciously received by him and invited to supper that evening.

To pass away the time before supper they were shown the sights of the city. The public buildings were so lofty that their roofs seemed to touch the sky, and the market-places were adorned with endless colonnades. Fountains of pure water, rose-water, and sugar-cane liqueur played unceasingly in the public squares, which were paved with a kind of precious stone smelling of cloves and cinnamon. Candide asked to see the Law Courts and the Court of

Appeal, but was told that there were none; court cases, in fact, were unknown. He enquired whether there were any prisons, and his guide answered no. What surprised and delighted him most of all was the Palace of Science, where he saw a gallery two thousand feet long filled with mathematical and scientific instruments.

The afternoon had passed, and they had seen little more than a thousandth part of the city, but it was time to go back to the royal palace for supper. Candide sat down to table with His Majesty, and Cacambo and several Court ladies were of the company. Never was entertainment so lavish as that supper party, and never was anyone so witty as His Majesty. Cacambo interpreted the King's witticisms to Candide, who found them still witty in translation, a point which surprised him as much as anything he heard or saw.

They spent a month at the palace, but not a day passed without Candide saying to Cacambo: 'It is quite true, my good fellow, that the house where I was born won't bear comparison with the mansions of this country; but still, I shall never be happy without Lady Cunégonde, and I dare say you have some mistress or other in Europe. If we stay here, we shall be no different from anybody else; but if we go back to the old world with a mere twelve sheep laden with Eldorado stones, we shall be richer than all the kings of Europe put together. We shall have nothing to fear from Inquisitors, and we shall easily rescue Lady Cunégonde.'

Cacambo was pleased at this, for, like Candide, he had a restless spirit. They were both anxious, also, to show their friends how rich they had grown and to boast about what they had seen in their travels. So these happy men decided to be happy no longer and to take leave of His Majesty.

'This is a foolish scheme of yours,' said the King; 'I realise that my country is not much to boast of, but a man should be satisfied with what works moderately well. I have no right to detain strangers against their will; that would be a tyranny which neither our customs nor our laws could justify. All men are free. Go when you wish, but you will find it difficult to get out. It is impossible to make your way against that torrent which so miraculously brought you here through subterranean caves. The mountains which surround my entire kingdom are ten thousand feet high, and as sheer as a wall. Each of them covers an area of more than thirty square miles, and when you reach the top, you can only clamber down precipices. However, since you are absolutely determined to leave, I will give orders to my engineers to make a machine to transport you in comfort. When you have been carried over the mountains, no one can accompany you any further; for my subjects have sworn never to cross the border, and they are too wise to break their oath. But apart from providing you with guides, you may ask me for anything you wish.'

'All we ask of Your Majesty,' said Cacambo, 'is a few sheep saddled with food and with the stones and mud of your country.'

The King laughed. 'I don't understand your European taste for our yellow mud,' he said; 'but take all you want, and much good may it do you.'

He immediately gave orders to his engineers to make a machine for hoisting these two extraordinary men out of his kingdom. Three thousand celebrated scientists set to work, and it was finished in fifteen days at a cost of not more than twenty thousand pounds sterling in the money of that country. Candide and Cacambo were placed on the machine with two large red sheep, saddled and bridled for riding after they had crossed the mountains, and in addition twenty sheep with pack-saddles full of food, thirty to carry exquisitely chosen presents, and fifty laden with gold, diamonds, and precious stones. Before they left, the King tenderly embraced the two wanderers.

Their departure was a beautiful sight, and the ingenious way in which they and their sheep were lifted over the tops of the mountains was worth watching. The scientists took leave of them after placing them in safety, and Candide had no other wish or object in view than to go and present his sheep to Lady Cunégonde.

'We can now pay off the Governor of Buenos Ayres,' he remarked, 'if Lady Cunégonde should be held to ransom. Let's go to Cayenne and set sail, and we will then see what kingdom we can buy.'

CHAPTER XIX

What happened to them at Surinam, and how Candide made the acquaintance of Martin

THE first day of their journey passed happily enough, for our two travellers were encouraged by the idea of seeing themselves owners of more treasure than Europe, Asia, and Africa could assemble; and, warmed by this vision, Candide wrote the name of Cunégonde on several trees. The second day two of their sheep plunged into a bog, and sank with all they carried; two more sheep died of fatigue a few days later, and seven or eight starved to death in the desert; some others fell down a precipice. After a hundred days' travelling only two sheep were left. Candide said to Cacambo:

'You see, my friend, how perishable are the riches of this world. There is nothing solid but virtue and the prospect of seeing Lady Cunégonde again.'

'I quite agree,' said Cacambo; 'but we have still got two sheep left with more treasure on their backs than the King of Spain will ever possess; and in the distance I see a town which I think must be Surinam. It belongs to the Dutch, you know. Our troubles are over, and happiness lies before us.'

As they were approaching the town, they noticed a negro lying full length at the side of the road and wearing nothing but a pair of blue canvas drawers. The poor fellow had no left leg and no right hand. Candide addressed him in Dutch:

'What are you doing here, my friend?' he asked. 'And what a dreadful state you are in!'

'I am waiting for my master, Mr. Vanderdendur, who owns the famous sugar-works,' replied the negro.

'Did Mr. Vanderdendur treat you like this?' asked Candide.

'Yes, Sir,' said the negro, 'it's the custom. For clothing, we are given a pair of canvas drawers twice a year. Those of us who work in the factories and happen to catch a finger in the grindstone have a hand chopped off; if we try to escape, they cut off one leg. Both accidents happened to me. That's the price of your eating sugar in Europe. My mother sold me on the coast of Guiana for fifty Spanish shillings. When she parted with me, she said: "Always honour and adore your fetishes, my dear boy, and they will make you happy; you have the honour of being a slave for milords the white men, and that is how you will make your parents' fortune." I don't know whether I made their fortune,' he continued, with a shake of his head, 'but they certainly did not make mine. Dogs, monkeys, and parrots are much less miserable than we are. The Dutch fetishes, who converted me, tell me every Sunday that we are all children of Adam, black and white alike. I am no genealogist; but if these preachers speak the truth, we must all be cousins. Now, you will surely agree that relations could not be treated more horribly.'

'Oh, Pangloss!' cried Candide. 'A scandal like this never occurred to you! But it's the truth, and I shall have to renounce that optimism of yours in the end.'

'What is optimism?' asked Cacambo.

'It's the passion for maintaining that all is right when all goes wrong with us,' replied Candide, weeping as he looked at the negro. And with tears in his eyes, he pursued his way to Surinam.

When they got there, the first enquiry they made was whether any ship in the harbour was going to Buenos Ayres. The man they spoke to happened to be a Spanish captain. He offered to make a deal, and suggested they should meet him at an inn to talk business; so Candide and the faithful Cacambo went to the rendezvous, taking their two sheep with them.

Candide, who always spoke as his heart dictated, told the Spaniard his adventures and announced that he wanted to rescue Lady Cunégonde.

'Then you won't get me to take you to Buenos Ayres,' said the captain. 'I should be hanged if I did, and so would you; for the lovely Cunégonde is My Lord's favourite mistress.'

This was a bitter blow to Candide, and he wept for a long time. At last he drew Cacambo aside and said to him:

'Now, my dear boy, this is what you must do. We have each of us five or six million diamonds in our pockets. You have a better head than I have. Go to Buenos Ayres and seize Lady Cunégonde. If the Governor makes any difficulties, give him a million; if he still protests, give him two. You haven't killed an Inquisitor, so you won't be suspected. I shall fit out another ship and go to Venice, where I shall wait for you. Venice is a free State where one has nothing to fear from Bulgars, Abars, Jews, and Inquisitors.'

Cacambo commended this wise plan. He was, of course, in despair at the idea of separation from a good master who had become his intimate friend, but the pleasure of being useful to him overcame his grief at leaving him. They embraced and shed some tears. Candide charged him not to forget the good old woman, and Cacambo left the same day. A most worthy fellow, Cacambo!

Candide stayed a little longer at Surinam while waiting for another ship's captain to take him and the two remaining sheep to Italy. He engaged some servants, and bought all that he needed for a long journey. At last, Mr. Vanderdendur, the master of a large ship, came and introduced himself.

'How much do you want,' Candide asked him, 'to take me to Venice directly? There's myself, my servants, my luggage, and those two sheep there.'

The captain suggested ten thousand piastres, and Candide agreed without hesitation.

'Oho!' said the prudent Vanderdendur to himself. 'This stranger is ready to give ten thousand piastres all at once, is he? He must be pretty rich.'

So he came back a moment later and intimated that he could not leave for less than twenty thousand.

'Very well,' said Candide. 'Twenty thousand be it.'

'Bless my soul,' said the captain, under his breath, 'this man is as ready to pay twenty thousand piastres as ten thousand.'

So he came back once more, and said he could not take him to Venice for less than thirty thousand piastres.

'Then you shall have thirty thousand,' replied Candide.

'So that's how the wind lies!' said the Dutch captain to himself once more. 'Thirty thousand piastres mean nothing to this man. No doubt the two sheep are loaded with immense treasures. We won't ask any more, but we will first make certain of the thirty thousand piastres, and then we'll see.'

Candide paid the captain in advance by selling two little diamonds, the smaller of which was worth more than all the money the captain asked. The two sheep were put on board, while Candide himself followed in a rowing-boat to join the ship which was lying at anchor in the roadstead. The captain watched his opportunity. He set his sails, raised anchor, and the wind favoured him. Candide beheld him in dismay and stupefaction, but the ship was soon lost to sight.

'Confound the fellow!' he cried. 'That's the sort of trick you would expect in the old world.'

He turned back to the shore, dejected with grief, for he had lost enough to make the fortune of twenty monarchs.

He went to call on a Dutch judge, and as he was a little distracted in mind, he knocked rudely on the door, entered, and recounted the adventure in rather louder tones than were altogether proper. The judge started by making him pay ten thousand piastres for the noise he had made. Then he listened patiently to him, and after promising that he would examine the affair as soon as the captain returned, made him pay a further ten thousand piastres to cover the expenses of the hearing.

This behaviour drove Candide to desperation. He had certainly experienced misfortunes a great deal more grievous; but the judge's indifference, and the coolness of the captain who had robbed him, affected his spleen and plunged him into the deepest melancholy. The wickedness of man appeared to him in all its ugliness, and his mind became a prey to gloomy thoughts. At last he found a French ship on the point of sailing for Bordeaux. As he had no more sheep loaded with diamonds to take on board, he engaged a berth at a reasonable price, and publicly announced that he would pay an honest man his board and passage and give him two thousand piastres to keep him company on the voyage, provided that the man was utterly dissatisfied with his condition and was the most unfortunate in the province.

So huge a crowd of candidates presented themselves that a fleet of ships would not have held them. To make his choice easier, Candide picked out some twenty people who looked sufficiently sociable, and who all claimed to deserve preference. After assembling them at his inn, he gave them supper on condition that each should take an oath to tell his story faithfully, and he promised to select the one who seemed to make the best case for having most to complain of and being most dissatisfied with his lot. The rest, he said, should receive consolation prizes.

The meeting lasted till four o'clock in the morning. While he listened to their adventures, Candide recollected what the old woman had said to him on their voyage to Buenos Ayres, and the bet she had made that there was no one on board who had not suffered grave misfortunes. He thought of Pangloss as each story was told, and said to himself:

'It would have puzzled the great man to make a good case for his theories. I wish he were here. If all goes well, it is in Eldorado, but nowhere else in the world.'

Candide decided at last in favour of a poor scholar who had done ten years' hack work for the Amsterdam publishers, his view being that there was no profession on earth with which a man should be more disgusted.

This scholar, who, for all that, was a very honest man, had been robbed by his wife, beaten by his son, and abandoned by his daughter, who had eloped with a Portuguese. He had lately been deprived of a small job on which he managed to live, and was persecuted by the clergy of Surinam on the grounds that he had denied the divinity of Christ. The other candidates admittedly were at least as unfortunate as he, but Candide hoped that a scholar would be the most likely to wile away the tedium of the voyage. The scholar's rivals all declared that Candide was doing them a great injustice, but he appeased them with a present of one hundred piastres each.

CHAPTER XX

What happened to Candide and Martin at sea

THUS the old scholar, whose name was Martin, embarked with Candide for Bordeaux. Both of them had seen and suffered much; and if the ship had been sailing from Surinam to Japan round the Cape of Good Hope, they could still have occupied the whole voyage discussing moral and physical evil.

Candide, however, had one great advantage over Martin, which was that he kept hoping to see Lady Cunégonde again, whereas Martin had nothing to hope for. Moreover, he still had some gold and diamonds left; and although he had lost a hundred large red sheep laden with the greatest treasures of the earth, and though he could not forget the knavery of the Dutch captain, he still inclined to Pangloss's philosophy whenever he recollected what he had in his pockets and remembered his Cunégonde.

'Now, tell me, Sir,' he said to the scholar, 'what do you think about it all? What is your opinion of moral and physical evil?'

'Sir,' replied Martin, 'the clergy of Surinam accused me of denying the divinity of Christ, but what I really believe is that man was created by the forces of evil and not by the forces of good.'

'You are jesting,' said Candide. 'People don't believe such things nowadays.'

'Well, here I am,' said Martin; 'I don't know what to do about it, but that's what I believe.'

'You must be possessed of the devil,' said Candide.

'He meddles so much with the affairs of this world,' replied Martin, 'that he may be living inside me, as well as everywhere else. But I confess that when I survey this globe, or rather this globule, I am forced to the conclusion that God has abandoned it to some mischievous power, though I make an exception of Eldorado, of course. I have scarcely seen a town which does not seek the ruin of a neighbouring town, nor a family that does not wish to exterminate some other family. You will find that the weak always detest the strong and cringe before them, and that the strong treat them like so many sheep to be sold for their meat and wool. A million regimented assassins surge from one end of Europe to the other, earning their living by committing murder and brigandage in strictest discipline, because they have no more honest livelihood; and in those towns which seem to enjoy the blessings of peace and where the arts flourish, men suffer more from envy, cares, and anxiety than a besieged town suffers from the scourges of war, for secret vexations are much more cruel than public miseries. In short, I have seen and experienced so much, that I am forced to believe that man's origin is evil.'

'All the same, there is some good,' replied Candide.

'Possibly,' said Martin, 'but I have never encountered it.'

In the middle of this discussion the noise of gunfire was heard, and grew louder at every moment. The ship's telescopes revealed two vessels fighting about three miles away; but the wind brought them both so close to the French ship, that the passengers had the pleasure of watching the fight in comfort. At last one of the ships fired a broadside which struck the other so squarely on the waterline that it sank to the bottom. Candide and Martin could distinctly see a hundred men on the deck of the sinking ship, their hands uplifted to heaven as they uttered the most terrible cries. A moment later they were swallowed under the sea.

'Well!' said Martin. 'You see how men treat each other!'

'There is certainly something diabolical about that,' said Candide.

As he was speaking, he noticed a bright red object swimming near his ship. A boat was lowered to see what it could be. It was one of his sheep. Candide felt more joy at recovering this sheep than all the grief he had suffered at losing the other hundred, each laden with large diamonds from Eldorado.

The French captain soon discovered that the captain of the victorious ship was a Spaniard, and that the defeated captain was a Dutch pirate; it was the same man, in fact, that had robbed Candide. The immense riches which this villain had stolen were swallowed up with him in the sea, and there was only one sheep saved.

'You observe,' said Candide to Martin, 'that crime is sometimes punished. That rogue of a Dutch captain has had the fate he deserved.'

'Yes,' said Martin. 'But why should the passengers have

perished too? God has punished a scoundrel, but the devil has drowned the rest.'

While the French ship and the Spaniard pursued their ways, Candide pursued his conversations with Martin. Their discussions lasted for a fortnight, and at the end of that time they had got no farther than when they had started; but they had had the pleasure of talking and exchanging ideas and consoling each other. Candide patted his sheep:

'Now that I have found you,' said he, 'I am sure I shall find my Cunégonde once more.'

CHAPTER XXI

What Candide and Martin discussed as they approached the coast of France

THE coast of France was sighted at last.

'Have you ever been to France, Sir?' asked Candide.

'Yes,' said Martin, 'I have travelled in several provinces. In some you find half the people are fools, and in others you find them much too subtle. There are some parts of the country where people are simple and stupid, and others where they pretend to be witty. But wherever you go in France, you will find that their three chief occupations are making love, backbiting, and talking nonsense.'

'But do you know Paris, Sir?' asked Candide.

'Oh, yes,' said Martin. 'I know Paris. You will find all sorts there. It's chaos, a mob of people all out for pleasure, and scarcely a soul who finds it. At least, that is how it appeared to me. I stayed there a short while: soon after I arrived I was robbed of all I had by some pickpockets at Saint Germain's Fair, and spent eight days in prison on suspicion of being a pickpocket myself. After that I took a job as a printer's reader to earn enough to pay my way back to Holland on foot. That is how I got to know the Grub Street hacks and every corner in the whole warren of intrigue and fanaticism. I am told that there are some people in that city noted for their good manners; I wish I could think so.'

'For my part,' said Candide, 'I have no curiosity to see France. You will appreciate that after spending a month in Eldorado, a man is not interested in seeing anything in the world except Lady Cunégonde. I am going to wait for her in Venice, and must cross France to reach Italy. You will keep me company, won't you?'

'Certainly,' said Martin. 'People say that Venice is no place to live in unless you are a Venetian nobleman, but that strangers are welcomed if they have plenty of money. I have none; but as you are well provided, I will follow you wherever you like to go.'

'By the way,' said Candide, 'do you agree with what they say in that big book the captain has, that the earth was originally all sea?'

'I no more believe it,' said Martin, 'than I believe all the other delirious ravings that are published from time to time.'

'But what was this world created for?' said Candide.

'To drive us mad,' replied Martin.

'You remember that story I told you,' continued

Candide, 'about the love of those two Oreillon girls for their monkeys. Doesn't that astonish you?'

'Not at all,' said Martin. 'I don't see anything strange in an infatuation like that. I have seen so many extraordinary things, that nothing is extraordinary any longer.'

'Do you think,' said Candide, 'that men have always massacred each other, as they do to-day, that they have always been false, cozening, faithless, ungrateful, thieving, weak, inconstant, mean-spirited, envious, greedy, drunken, miserly, ambitious, bloody, slanderous, debauched, fanatic, hypocritical, and stupid?'

'Do you think,' said Martin, 'that hawks have always eaten pigeons when they could find them?'

'Of course I do,' said Candide.

'Well,' said Martin, 'if hawks have always had the same character, why should you suppose that men have changed theirs?'

'Oh, but there's a great difference,' said Candide; 'for Free Will . . .'

They were still talking when the ship reached Bordeaux.

CHAPTER XXII

What happened to Candide and Martin in France

CANDIDE stopped in Bordeaux only long enough to sell a few Eldorado pebbles and buy himself a handsome carriage with two seats, for he found he could not do without Martin, his philosopher. The only thing which annoyed him was parting company with his sheep. He left it to the Academy of Sciences at Bordeaux, who set for the subject of their annual prize an essay on why the sheep's fleece was red. The prize was awarded to a Northern scholar, who demonstrated by a formula, A plus B minus C over Z, that the sheep was necessarily red and ought to die of scab.

It so happened that all the travellers Candide met at the inns on the road told him they were going to Paris. Such general eagerness eventually decided him to see the capital for himself, especially as this would not involve much detour from the road to Venice.

He entered by the Saint Marceau suburb, and thought he must be in the filthiest village in Westphalia.

Scarcely had Candide reached his hotel, when he was attacked by a slight illness caused by the exertions of the journey. As he wore an enormous diamond ring on his finger, and a prodigiously heavy cash-box had been noticed amongst his luggage, he was soon attended by two doctors whom he had not sent for, some intimate friends who would not leave him, and two ladies given to good works who saw that his broth was properly warmed. Martin remarked:

'I remember being ill myself during my first visit to Paris. I was very poor. But then I had no friends, no kind ladies, and no doctors, so I soon recovered.'

By dint of medicines and bleeding, Candide's disorder now became serious. The parish priest called, and politely asked him for a note from his confessor payable to the bearer in the other world. Candide would have nothing to do with it. The two ladies assured him that it was a new custom, but Candide replied that he was not a man of fashion. Martin threatened to throw the priest out of the window, and he on his part swore that he would never bury Candide. Martin swore that he would bury the priest, if he pestered them any longer. The dispute grew more and more heated, until at last Martin took the priest by the shoulders and sent him packing. This caused great offence, and a law-suit was started.

Candide began to mend, and during his convalescence had some fashionable people to supper, who played cards with him for high stakes. It astonished Candide that he never held an ace in his hand, but Martin was not surprised.

Amongst those who showed him the sights of the town was a spry little *abbé* from Périgord, obliging, fawning, and as bold as brass, yet useful in his way. He was one of those busybodies who lie in wait for strangers passing through Paris, and tell them all the tittle-tattle of the town, while offering them entertainment at any price. This fellow first of all took Candide and Martin to the theatre, where a new tragedy was being acted. Candide happened to be sitting near a party of wits, but that did not prevent him from weeping when scenes which affected him were beautifully acted. One of these critics, who was sitting in the next seat, turned to him during the interval, and remarked:

'You are quite wrong to weep. That actress is very bad, and the actor playing with her is worse still. The play is even worse than the actors. The author does not know one word of Arabic, yet the scene is set in Arabia! And what is more, he doesn't believe in innate ideas. To-morrow I'll bring you twenty reviews of his work, and all hostile.'

Candide turned to the *abbé*:

'How many plays have been written in French?' he asked.

'About five or six thousand,' replied the *abbé*.

'That's a lot,' he remarked; 'how many are good?'

'Fifteen or sixteen,' replied the other.

'That's a lot,' said Martin.

Candide was delighted with the performance of an actress who took the part of Queen Elizabeth in a rather insipid tragedy which is sometimes performed.

'That actress is charming,' said he to Martin; 'she reminds me of Lady Cunégonde; I should like to pay her my respects.'

The *abbé* offered to introduce him to her at her own house. As Candide had been brought up in Germany, he began to make enquiries about etiquette, and asked how the queens of England are treated in France.

'It depends where you are,' said the *abbé*. 'In the provinces, people take them to an inn; in Paris, they treat them with great respect while they are still beautiful, but when they are dead they throw them on the dunghill.'

'Queens thrown on the dunghill!' exclaimed Candide.

'Yes, indeed,' said Martin. 'Our friend here is quite right. I was in Paris when Monimia passed, as they say, from this life to the other. She was refused what people call "a decent funeral"—that is to say, being sent to rot with all the parish beggars in some filthy cemetery. She was buried away from all her people at the corner of Burgundy Street. It must have given her a shock, for she had exalted ideas of what is proper.'

'But surely that was most impolite behaviour,' said Candide.

'What can you expect?' said Martin. 'That's how people here are made. Imagine every possible contradiction and inconsistency, and you will find them in the government, the law-courts, the churches, and in the whole life of this absurd nation.'

'Is it true,' asked Candide, 'that people in Paris are always laughing?'

'Yes,' said the *abbé*, 'but they are laughing with vexation; for they complain of everything with loud bursts of laughter, just as they laugh while they commit the most detestable crimes.'

'Who was that ill-mannered creature,' said Candide, 'who spoke so harshly of the play at which I wept so freely, and of the actors who gave me such pleasure?'

'He's an evil-minded fellow,' said the *abbé*, 'who earns his living by damning every play and every book. He hates a successful writer, just as eunuchs hate successful lovers. He is one of those snakes of literature who feed on dirt and venom. He's a pamphleteer.'

'What do you mean by a pamphleteer?' asked Candide.

'A dealer in odd sheets of paper,' replied the *abbé*, 'a journalist.'

Such was Candide's conversation with Martin and the *abbé* as they stood on the staircase after the performance, watching the rest of the audience stream past them.

'Eager as I am to see Lady Cunégonde once more,' said Candide, 'I should like to have supper with Mademoiselle Clairon, for her acting greatly took my fancy.'

The *abbé* was not the right man to ask for an introduction to Mademoiselle Clairon, who moved only in the best society.

'She has an engagement for this evening,' said he; 'but

allow me the honour of presenting you to a lady of quality, in whose house you will quickly gain four years' experience of Parisian life.'

Candide, who was curious by nature, let himself be taken to call on the lady, who lived in the Saint Honoré suburb. A game of faro was in progress when they arrived. Twelve melancholy punters each held a little heap of cards, which they had dog-eared to register their misfortunes. Deep silence reigned, which seemed to emphasise the pallor of the punters' faces and the anxiety of the banker. The lady of the house was seated near this pitiless banker, and kept her lynx-eyes trained on all the double-stakes with which each player dog-eared his cards. She made them turn the corners back with a glance which, though severe, was polite and inoffensive for fear of losing her clients. The lady had taken the title of Marchioness of Doublestakesworthy. Her daughter, aged fifteen, sat with the punters, and indicated by a wink of her eye whenever any of the poor creatures attempted to repair the cruelties of Fortune by cheating. The *abbé*, Candide, and Martin entered the room, but no one rose or took any notice of them; all were too deeply occupied with their cards.

'The Baroness of Thunder-ten-tronckh had much better manners,' said Candide.

The *abbé*, however, whispered in the Marchioness's ear, and she thereupon raised herself in her chair, and honoured Candide with a gracious smile and Martin with a dignified nod of her head. Candide was then shown to a seat and handed a pack of cards, with which he lost fifty thousand francs in two deals. After this episode they adjourned for supper in good spirits, and everyone was astonished that

Candide was not moved by his loss. The footmen said to each other in their peculiar jargon:

'This must be one of those English milords.'

The supper was like most Parisian suppers, first of all silence followed by an indistinguishable noise of words, then some witticisms, most of which were insipid, some scandal, some false reasoning, a little politics and a good deal of slander. Some new books happened to be mentioned.

'Have you seen that novel of Dr. Gauchat's?' said the *abbé*.

'Yes,' said one of the guests, 'but I couldn't finish it. There is a great deal of pointless stuff published to-day, but none of it approaches Gauchat for sheer impertinence. I have become so tired of this flood of detestable books which deluges us nowadays, that I have taken to punting at faro.'

'And Canon T.'s essays?' said the *abbé*. 'What do you think of them?'

'Oh! What a bore he is!' exclaimed Lady Doublestakesworthy. 'What pains he takes to tell you what everyone knows! What ponderous discussions about things which are not worth even a casual remark! He is always stealing other people's witticisms and missing the point in the process. He spoils everything he pilfers. I am sick to death of him! But he won't sicken me any longer; for a few pages of the Canon are quite enough for anyone.'

Seated at the table was a man of some taste and learning who supported the Marchioness's remarks. The discussion then passed to tragedy, and the lady asked how it was that tragedies were sometimes acted which no one could bear to read. The man of taste explained clearly how a play

could interest an audience and yet have very little merit.
He proved in a few words that it is not enough to collect
from any novel one or two of those situations which will
always enchant an audience: a dramatist must have ideas
which are fresh without being fantastic; he must be able to
touch the sublime yet remain natural; and he must know
the human heart and make it speak. He must be a great
poet, without representing any of his characters as a poet.
He must understand the language perfectly and speak it
purely and harmoniously, yet he must never allow the
rhyme to dictate the meaning.

'Whoever infringes any of these rules,' he added, 'may
write one or two tragedies which will be applauded in the
theatre, but he will never be reckoned a good writer. There
are very few good tragedies. Some are pretty little things,
quite well written in their way. Some are political argu-
ments which send us to sleep. Some are revolting amplifica-
tions of some simple theme. And some are the expressions
of wild frenzy, written in the crudest style, and full of
desultory talk, long addresses to the gods (for want of
knowing how to speak to men), false observations, and
turgid commonplaces.'

Candide listened attentively to these remarks, and con-
ceived a high opinion of the speaker; and as the Marchion-
ess had taken care that he should sit beside her, he took the
liberty of whispering in her ear and asking who this person
was that spoke so well.

'He is a scholar, who never plays faro,' said the lady, 'but
the *abbé* sometimes brings him here for supper. He is well
read in tragedies and other books, and has himself written a
tragedy which was hissed on performance and a book

which has never been seen outside his bookseller's shop, except for one copy he sent to me with a dedication.'

'Yes, undoubtedly a great man!' said Candide. 'He is another Pangloss.'

Then, turning towards him, Candide said:

'No doubt you think, Sir, that all is for the best in the physical and moral world, and that things could not be otherwise?'

'For my part, Sir,' replied the scholar, 'I think nothing of the sort. I find that all goes wrong with us, and that no one knows his place in society or his proper employment. Except at supper parties, which are lively enough and where people appear to be in some measure of agreement, our time is spent in pointless quarrels, Jansenists against Molinists, Parliament against Church, men of letters against men of letters, one clique at court against another, big business against the people, wives against their husbands, kinsmen against kinsmen. In fact, it is perpetual civil war.'

'I have seen worse,' replied Candide. 'But a wise man, who has since had the misfortune to be hanged, taught me that there is a marvellous propriety in such things; they are the shadows in a beautiful picture.'

'Your friend that was hanged had his joke at the world's expense,' said Martin; 'those shadows you speak of are horrible blemishes.'

'The blemishes are made by men,' said Candide, 'who cannot do otherwise.'

'Then it is not their fault,' said Martin.

The majority of the punters, who could not understand this discussion, sat by drinking, while Martin argued with the scholar, and Candide told some of his adventures to the lady of the house.

After supper, the Marchioness took Candide to her private room and led him to a couch.

'So you are still devoted to the Lady Cunégonde de Thunder-ten-Tronckh?' she asked.

'Yes, madam,' answered Candide.

The Marchioness replied with a tender smile:

'You answer me like a young man from Westphalia. A Frenchman would have said, "It is true that I once loved Lady Cunégonde; but on seeing you, madam, I find I love her no more."'

'Very well, Madam,' said Candide, 'I will answer as you wish.'

'Your passion for her,' continued the Marchioness, 'started from the moment you picked up her handkerchief. Be so good as to pick up my garter.'

'With all my heart,' said Candide, picking it up.

'And now I shall be glad if you will replace it for me,' said the lady; and Candide replaced it for her.

'You are, of course, a stranger here,' said the lady. 'I sometimes make my Parisian lovers languish for a fortnight; but here I am, surrendering myself to you on the very first evening, because it is right to pay the honours of one's country to a young man from Westphalia.'

The charmer noticed two enormous diamonds on the young stranger's two hands, and praised them so earnestly that from Candide's fingers they passed to the fingers of the Marchioness.

As he went back to his hotel with the *abbé*, Candide felt some remorse at his infidelity to Lady Cunégonde. The *abbé* noticed his uneasiness, and suited himself to Candide's mood. He had had only a small share in the fifty thousand francs Candide had lost at cards, and of the value of the two diamonds which the Marchioness had wheedled from him. His intention was to make as much profit as he could procure from his knowledge of Candide, so he talked much to him about Cunégonde, and Candide told him that he would beg that charmer's pardon for his infidelity, when he should see her at Venice.

The *abbé* redoubled his polite attentions, and took a tender interest in all Candide said and did, and in all he intended to do.

'So you have arranged to meet Lady Cunégonde at Venice, Sir?' said the *abbé*.

'Yes, Sir,' replied Candide. 'It is essential for me to go and find Lady Cunégonde.'

And so, being absorbed in the pleasure of talking about what he loved, he told (as his custom was) part of his adventures with that illustrious Westphalian lady.

'I should think,' said the *abbé*, 'that Lady Cunégonde must be very witty. Her letters must be charming.'

'I have never had any,' said Candide; 'for after being driven from the house because of my passion, you can well imagine that I could not write to her. Shortly afterwards I learned that she was dead; then I found her again and lost her once more, and now I have sent a messenger to where she lives four thousand five hundred miles from here, and am waiting for an answer.'

The *abbé* listened attentively and seemed to be musing. Soon after he tenderly embraced the two strangers and took his leave. The following day, when Candide awoke, he received a letter worded as follows:

'My dearest love, I have been lying ill for a whole week in this town. News has just reached me that you are here, and I would fly to your arms if I could move. I learned of your voyage to Bordeaux, and have left the faithful Cacambo and the old woman there. They should soon be following me. The Governor of Buenos Ayres took everything, but your heart is still mine. Do come. Your presence will bring me back to life, or make me die of pleasure.'

This charming and unexpected letter gave Candide inexpressible joy, though the illness of his dear Cunégonde dejected him with grief. Torn between these two passions, he took his gold and his diamonds and drove with Martin to the hotel where Lady Cunégonde was staying. He entered her room trembling with emotion, his heart beating, and his voice choked with sobs. He stretched out a hand to draw aside the bed curtains and to lighten the room.

'Be careful what you are doing,' said the nurse. 'The light will kill her,' and she drew the curtain back.

'My dear Cunégonde,' said Candide, weeping, 'how are you, my darling? If you cannot see me, speak to me at least.'

'She cannot speak,' said the nurse.

The woman then drew from the bed a plump hand, which Candide first grasped and bathed with tears before covering it with diamonds. He then placed a bag full of gold on the armchair.

In the midst of his transports an officer arrived, followed by the *abbé* and an escort.

'Are those the two suspicious strangers?' said the officer;

and he immediately gave his minions orders to seize them
and put them in prison.

'This is not the way travellers are treated in Eldorado,'
said Candide.

'I am more than ever convinced that man is evil,' said
Martin.

'But where are you taking us, Sir?' asked Candide.

'To a dungeon,' said the officer.

As Martin recovered his composure, he realised that the
lady who pretended to be Cunégonde was a fraud, that the
abbé who had so rapidly taken advantage of Candide's
innocence was also a fraud, and the officer another fraud
who could easily be got rid of.

He therefore gave some advice which Candide readily
accepted, since he had no wish to be exposed to a law-suit
and was, besides, as impatient as ever to see the real Cuné-
gonde again. Accordingly Candide showed the officer
three little diamonds, each worth about three thousand
pistoles.

'Good God, Sir,' said the man with the ivory truncheon,
'if you had committed every crime imaginable, you would
still be the most honest man in the world. Three diamonds!
Each worth three thousand pistoles! My dear Sir, I would
rather die than take you to prison. All strangers are under
arrest; but leave it to me, Sir, leave it to me. I have a
brother at Dieppe in Normandy. I will bring you there,
and if you have a diamond or so to give him, he will take
just as good care of you.'

'But why are all strangers under arrest?' said Candide.

It was the *abbé* who replied. 'The reason is,' said he, 'that a
beggar from Artois heard some people talking nonsense,

and this led him to commit a murder. It was not murder after the fashion of May 1610, but after the fashion of December 1594 and of several other murders committed in other years and other months by other beggars who had heard people talking nonsense.'

The officer explained what the *abbé* meant.

'How monstrous!' cried Candide. 'Do you mean to say that such horrors are committed by a people so fond of dancing and singing! I could not escape too quickly from a land where monkeys worry tigers. I have seen bears in my own country, but I have never seen men except in Eldorado. For Heaven's sake, Officer, take me to Venice, where I have to wait for Lady Cunégonde.'

'I can only take you to Lower Normandy,' said the Chief Yeoman of the Guard.

He thereupon ordered the handcuffs to be removed, and remarking that he had been mistaken, he dismissed his escort and took Candide and Martin to Dieppe, where he left them in the hands of his brother. A small Dutch vessel was lying in the harbour. Three diamonds helped to make the Norman the most obliging of men, and a passage was arranged for Candide and his retinue on board the ship, which was leaving for Portsmouth in England. It was not the road to Venice; but Candide felt that he had been delivered from Hell, and reckoned that he could resume his way to Venice at the first opportunity.

CHAPTER XXIII

Candide and Martin reach the coast of England, and what they see there

'Oh, Martin, Martin!' cried Candide to his friend, as they stood side by side on board the Dutch vessel, 'to think of Pangloss and my dear Cunégonde, and all that has happened to them! What do you make of this world of ours?'

'I find it a senseless and detestable piece of work,' replied Martin.

'You know England,' continued Candide, after a pause, 'are they as mad there as they are in France?'

'Yes,' said Martin, 'but theirs is another kind of folly. You realise, of course, that these two nations are fighting over a few acres of snow on the borders of Canada, and that they spend more money on this glorious war than the whole of Canada is worth. To decide whether there are more people who ought to be locked up in one country than in the other exceeds my feeble powers; I only know that by and large the people we are going to visit have a most serious and gloomy temperament.'

While they were talking, the ship reached Portsmouth. The waterside was crowded with a host of people who were gazing intently at a stout man kneeling, with his eyes bandaged, on the deck of a man of war. Four soldiers stood opposite him and fired three rounds each into his skull with the utmost composure, at which the crowd dispersed evidently quite satisfied.

'What can all this be about?' cried Candide, 'and what evil is it that rules the roast here and everywhere?'

He asked who the stout man was who had just been so ceremoniously disposed of.

'He was an admiral,' they told him.

'But why execute this admiral?' he enquired.

'Because he had not enough dead men to his credit,' was the reply; 'he joined battle with a French admiral, and it has been established that their ships were not close enough to engage.'

'But surely,' exclaimed Candide, 'the French admiral must have been just as far from the English as the English admiral was from the French!'

'True enough,' was the answer; 'but in this country we find it pays to shoot an admiral from time to time to encourage the others.'

Candide was so taken aback at what he had seen and heard that he refused even to set foot on English soil, and made a bargain with the Dutch captain to take him to Venice without delay, even though the man might cheat him as the fellow from Surinam had done.

After two days the captain was ready. They coasted France, and sailed within sight of Lisbon, at which Candide shuddered. They entered the straits, passed into the Mediterranean and at last anchored at Venice.

'Heaven be praised,' cried Candide, embracing Martin: 'this is where I shall see my lovely Cunégonde again. I trust Cacambo as I would trust myself. All is well; we're in the right road now, and the outlook is as fine as possible.'

CHAPTER XXIV

About Pacquette and Brother Giroflée

As soon as they reached Venice, the search for Cacambo began. Candide tried every inn and restaurant, and visited every woman of the streets, but Cacambo was not to be found. He had every ship watched as the passengers disembarked, but still no news of Cacambo.

'Look at the time I have spent,' said Candide to Martin. 'I have been from Surinam to Bordeaux, from Bordeaux to Paris, from Paris to Dieppe, and from Dieppe to Portsmouth. I have sailed down the coasts of Spain and Portugal, I have crossed the Mediterranean and have spent several months at Venice, and still my lovely Cunégonde has not arrived. The only people I have met instead of her have been a shameless hussy and an *abbé* from Périgord. There's no doubt about it, Cunégonde is dead, and I may as well die, too. How much better off I should have been to stay in Eldorado, which seemed like Paradise, instead of returning to this confounded Europe! How right you are, my dear Martin! There is nothing here but illusion and one calamity after another.'

He sank into a deep melancholy, and would have nothing to do with the opera and other amusements of the carnival. And as far as ladies were concerned, he was not in the least danger of temptation.

'You surely are a simple fellow,' said Martin, 'to believe that a mongrel servant, with five or six millions in his pocket, will go looking for your mistress to the ends of the earth and bring her here to Venice for you. He'll take her for himself, if he finds her; and if he doesn't, he'll take another. My advice is to forget your Cacambo and your Cunégonde.'

Martin's words gave no consolation. Candide's melancholy increased, while Martin kept on proving to him that there is little virtue and little happiness in the world, except perhaps in Eldorado, where no one could go.

One day, while they were discussing this important subject and waiting for Cunégonde, Candide noticed a young monk in St. Mark's Square arm in arm with a girl. The monk looked a plump, robust, rosy-cheeked fellow. His manner was confident, and there was an air of pride in every step he took. The girl was pretty. As she walked along she sang, casting amorous glances at her monk and pinching his fat cheeks from time to time.

'You will at least allow,' said Candide to Martin, 'that these two are happy. Up to now I have met only the unlucky wherever I have been, except in Eldorado; but I will take a bet that this girl and her monk are happy enough.'

'Right!' said Martin. 'I accept the bet.'

'All we have to do, then,' said Candide, 'is to invite them to dinner, and you will see if I am wrong.'

He immediately accosted them, and presenting his compliments, invited them to his inn to eat macaroni, Lombardy pheasant, and caviar, and to drink Montepulciano, Lacrima Christi, and the wines of Cyprus and Samos. The young lady blushed; but as the monk accepted the invitation, she followed him, glancing at Candide in astonishment and confusion, and with tears starting to her eyes. She had scarcely entered Candide's room when she remarked:

'So you don't recognise Pacquette any longer, Master Candide?'

Candide had been too much occupied with thoughts of Cunégonde to pay her much attention, but at these words he exclaimed:

'My poor child! So it's you—the girl who got Dr Pangloss into such a pretty mess!'

'Yes, sir,' said Pacquette, 'I am afraid so, and I see you know all about it. I heard of the dreadful things which happened to my Lady's household and to the lovely Cunégonde, but I assure you that my experiences have been scarcely less sad. I was an innocent little girl when you first saw me, so a friar who was my confessor had little difficulty in seducing me. The consequences were horrible. I was forced to leave the house soon after my Lord had sent you packing with powerful kicks on the behind, and if a famous doctor had not taken pity on me, I should have died. For some time I was the doctor's mistress out of sheer gratitude; but his wife, who was violently jealous, used to beat me unmercifully every day. What a fury she was! The doctor was the ugliest man you ever saw, and I was the most wretched creature alive being continually beaten for the sake of a man I did not love. You know, sir, how dangerous it is for a cross-grained woman to marry a doctor. Her husband was driven to distraction by her behaviour; so one day he gave her a medicine for a slight cold, which proved so efficacious that she died within two hours in horrible convulsions. Her relations prosecuted him, and he was forced to flee; so they put me in prison.

instead. My innocence would not have saved me, if I had not been moderately pretty. The judge released me on condition that he succeeded the doctor, but I was soon supplanted by a rival and dismissed without a penny in my pocket. That is how I have been forced to continue in this detestable way of life, which to you men seems so pleasing, but to us is nothing but a hell of suffering. I came to Venice to practise my profession. Oh, sir, if you could only imagine what it means to be obliged to fondle a retired business man, a lawyer, a monk, a gondolier, or an *abbé* with the same show of affection, to be exposed to every insult and humiliation, to be reduced to borrowing a skirt for some disagreeable creature to lift up, to be robbed by one man of what one has earned with another, to be fleeced by the magistrates, and to have no prospect in view but a terrible old age, the workhouse, and the dunghill, you would realise that I am one of the most unhappy creatures alive.'

Pacquette had been opening her heart to the worthy Candide as they sat in his private room. Martin, who had listened to every word, said to Candide:

'You see! I have already won half the bet.'

Brother Giroflée had stopped in the dining-room to take a drink before dinner.

'But you were looking so gay and happy when I met you,' said Candide to Pacquette; 'you were singing and fondling the monk in a most natural and affectionate manner. You seemed as happy as you now pretend to be unfortunate.'

'That, sir,' said Pacquette, with a sigh, 'is one more misery of this way of life. Yesterday I was robbed and beaten by an officer, and to-day I must appear good-humoured to please a monk.'

This was enough for Candide. He acknowledged that Martin was right, and both sat down to table with the monk and Pacquette. The dinner went well, and by the end they were talking quite freely.

'Father,' said Candide to the monk, 'it seems to me that everyone should envy your good luck. You look the picture of health, and your face shows how happy you are. You have a pretty girl for your recreation, and you seem contented with your condition in the Church.'

'Believe me, sir,' said Brother Giroflée, 'I should be glad if my whole order were at the bottom of the sea. I have been tempted again and again to set the monastery on fire and turn Turk. My parents forced me to put on this detestable garb at the age of fifteen so as to leave a larger fortune to a confounded elder brother, curse him! As for the monastery, it is riddled with jealousy, discord, and fury. I admit that some miserable sermons I have preached have brought me in a little money, though the Prior robs me of half of it; at any rate I am left enough to pay for my girls. But when I return to the monastery in the evening, I feel inclined to break my head against the dormitory walls; and all my brother monks feel exactly the same.'

Martin turned to Candide: 'Well,' said he, with his customary composure, 'haven't I won the whole bet?'

Candide gave Pacquette two thousand piastres and Brother Giroflée one thousand.

'My reply to you,' said he, 'is that that will make them happy.'

'I don't believe anything of the kind,' said Martin. 'It

would not surprise me if those piastres of yours made them even more unhappy.'

'Well, come what may,' said Candide, 'one thing comforts me. I find that a man often meets people that he never expected to see again. It may well happen that since my red sheep and Pacquette have turned up, I shall also meet Cunégonde once more.'

'I hope,' said Martin, 'that one day she will make you happy, but I very much doubt it.'

'What a pessimist you are!' exclaimed Candide.

'That is because I know what life is,' said Martin.

'Just look at those gondoliers!' said Candide. 'Do they ever stop singing?'

'You don't see them at home with their wives and their little brats,' said Martin. 'The Doge has his troubles, and the gondoliers have theirs. I admit that on the whole the gondolier's lot is preferable to the Doge's, but the difference seems to me so small that it is not worth examining.'

'People talk of the senator, Pococurante,' said Candide, 'who lives in that beautiful palace on the Brenta, and receives strangers so courteously. They say he is a man who has never known what worry is.'

'I should like to see such a rare specimen, said Martin.

Candide immediately sent to ask Count Pococurante's permission to visit him the following day.

CHAPTER XXV

A visit to Count Pococurante, a noble Venetian

CANDIDE and Martin took a gondola and were rowed down the Brenta to the palace of the noble Pococurante. The gardens were elegantly laid out and ornamented with beautiful marble statues, and the palace was a gem of architecture. The master of the house, a man of sixty and extremely rich, received the two travellers quite politely, but without much warmth, at which Candide was disconcerted. Martin, however, was not at all displeased.

After an exchange of greetings, two pretty girls, neatly dressed, served them with cups of frothy chocolate. Candide could not help exclaiming at their beauty, their style, and their manner.

'They suit me well enough,' said Count Pococurante. 'I sometimes take them to bed with me, for I am so tired of the ladies of the town with their flirtations, their jealousies, their quarrels, their moods, their trivialities, their pride, their stupidities, and the sonnets we have to make or order for them. But I find that I am getting tired of these two girls as well.'

After this refreshment, Candide strolled into the long gallery, and was struck with the beauty of the pictures. He asked who had painted the first two.

'They are by Raphael,' said the senator; 'I was vain enough to pay a high price for them some years ago. They are said to be two of the most beautiful in Italy, but they give me no pleasure at all. The colour is altogether dull, and there is not enough modelling in the figures, which do not stand out sufficiently. Besides, the draperies bear not the least resemblance to cloth. In short, whatever others say, I fail to discover in them a true imitation of Nature. I only enjoy a painting when I fancy I see Nature itself, and there are scarcely any of that kind to be found. I have plenty of pictures, but I no longer look at them.'

While waiting for dinner, Pococurante had a concerto performed. Candide found the music enchanting.

'This noise,' said Pococurante, 'can give half an hour's amusement; but if it lasts any longer it bores everyone, though no one dares to admit it. Music to-day is nothing more than the art of performing difficult pieces, and what is merely difficult gives no lasting pleasure.

'I might perhaps have preferred opera if it had not developed into a monstrosity that utterly disgusts me. It does not matter to me if people go to see bad tragedies set to music, where the scenes merely provide inappropriate occasions for two or three ridiculous songs to exhibit the quality of an actress's throat. And if a man can experience transports of pleasure on seeing a eunuch warbling the part of Caesar or Cato and strutting awkwardly across the stage, then let him enjoy it by all means. But for my part, I have long ceased to attend such wretched entertainment, though it is the glory of modern Italy and the expensive plaything of kings.'

Candide argued a little, but he argued discreetly. Martin entirely agreed with the senator.

They sat down to table, and, after an excellent dinner, withdrew to the library. Candide noticed a Homer magnificently bound, and complimented the nobleman on his good taste.

'There is a book,' said he, 'which used to delight our great Pangloss, the most renowned philosopher of Germany.'

'It doesn't delight me,' said Pococurante coldly; 'there was a time when people convinced me that I enjoyed reading Homer; but that eternal succession of identical combats, those gods who are always so busy to no effect, that Helen of his who gives rise to the war yet plays so little part in the story, that Troy so endlessly besieged without being taken—it bores me to distraction! I have sometimes asked learned men if they found this book as tedious as I do. Those who were sincere all confessed that it dropped from their hands, but that they felt obliged to keep it in their library, like a relic of the past or like rusty coins with no current use.'

'Your Excellency can hardly think the same of Virgil,' said Candide.

'I admit,' said Pococurante, 'that the second, fourth, and sixth books of his *Aeneid* are excellent; but as for his pious Aeneas, and his brave Cloanthus, and his faithful Achates, and his little Ascanius, and that feeble king Latinus, his coarse Amata, and the insipid Lavinia, I think there is nothing more frigid or more displeasing. I prefer Tasso and the rigmaroles of Ariosto.'

'Should I be correct, Sir,' said Candide, 'in assuming that you find pleasure in reading Horace?'

'There are some maxims,' said Pococurante, 'by which a man of the world can profit, and since they are expressed in forceful verse, they are the more easily committed to memory. But I care little for his visit to Brundisium, and his description of a bad dinner, and the Billingsgate quarrel between some fellow Pupilus, "whose words", as he says, "were full of pus", and another whose words "were as sour as vinegar". I read with extreme displeasure the coarse verses against old women and witches; and I cannot detect what merit there can be in saying to his friend, Mæcenas, that if he will only place him in the ranks of lyric poets, he will touch the stars with his exalted head. Fools admire everything in an established classic. I read only to please myself, and enjoy only what suits my taste.'

Candide was astonished at what he heard, for he had been brought up never to exercise his own judgment. Martin, however, found Pococurante's way of thinking quite reasonable.

'Oh,' said Candide, 'here is a Cicero. A great man like that I feel sure you never grow tired of reading.'

'I never read him at all,' replied the Venetian; 'what does it matter to me that he pleaded for Rabirius or Cluentius? I have enough cases of my own to try. I used to prefer his philosophical works; but when I found that he was in doubt about everything, I decided that I knew as much as he and needed no one's help to remain ignorant.'

'I notice eighty volumes here of the proceedings of a scientific academy,' said Martin; 'amongst so many there may be something interesting.'

'There would be,' said Pococurante, 'if even one of the authors of this farrago had invented no more than the art of making pins; but these collections merely consist of vain philosophical systems, devoid of any useful information.'

'That's a fine collection of plays I see there . . .' said Candide. 'Italian, Spanish, French. . . .'

'Yes,' said the senator, 'there are three thousand of them, and not three dozen are any good. . . . As for these collections of sermons which all told are not worth a page of Seneca, and these fat volumes of theology, you will readily believe that they are never opened by me or by anyone else.'

Martin noticed some shelves filled with English books.

'Most of these works,' said he, 'will no doubt appeal to a republican, since they are written with such a sense of freedom.'

'Yes,' replied Pococurante, 'it is fine to write what one thinks; it is the privilege of man. In Italy what we write we never think. Those who live in the country of the Caesars and the Antonines dare not entertain an idea without the permission of a cleric. . . . But I should be better pleased by the liberty which inspires these English masters, if the violence of party spirit did not corrupt all that is valuable in it.'

Candide noticed a Milton, and asked if he allowed the greatness of that author.

'Milton?' said Pococurante; 'that barbarian who made a tedious commentary on the first chapter of Genesis in ten books of rugged verse? That clumsy imitator of the Greeks, who disfigures the creation and, instead of representing the Eternal Being, as Moses does, creating the universe at a word, makes the Messiah take a large pair of compasses from one of the cupboards of Heaven to draw a plan of his intended work? Do you expect me to appreciate the man who has spoiled Tasso's conception of Hell and the Devil, who disguises Lucifer first as a toad and then as a pigmy, who makes him repeat the same speeches a hundred times, and even argue about theology? Why, the man has so little humour as to imitate in all seriousness Ariosto's comic invention of firearms and make the devils fire cannons in Heaven! Neither I nor anyone else in Italy can take pleasure in these sorry extravagances. The marriage of Sin and Death and the snakes to which Sin gives birth sicken every man with any delicacy of taste, and his long description of a hospital will only please a gravedigger. This obscure, bizarre, and disagreeable poem was despised on publication. I judge it to-day as it was first judged by the author's fellow-countrymen. I say what I think, and care little whether others agree with me.'

Candide was distressed at these remarks, for he admired Homer and was quite fond of Milton.

'I am much afraid,' he whispered to Martin, with a shake of his head, 'that this man would have a supreme contempt for our German poets.'

'There would be no harm in that,' replied Martin.

'What a superior man!' murmured Candide. 'What a genius this Pococurante is! Nothing can please him.'

When they had glanced over all the books, they went down to the garden. Candide began to admire its beauties.

'I know nothing in such bad taste,' said the owner; 'it consists entirely of trifling conceits. But to-morrow I intend to have a garden laid out on a nobler design.'

After the visitors had taken leave of his Excellency, Candide said to Martin:

'You must admit that there is the happiest man alive, because he is superior to all he possesses.'

'Don't you see,' said Martin, 'that he is disgusted with everything he possesses? Plato long ago said that the best stomachs are not those that reject all food.'

'But,' said Candide, 'isn't there a pleasure in criticising everything and discovering faults where other men detect beauties?'

'That is to say,' replied Martin, 'that there is a pleasure in not being pleased.'

'Never mind,' said Candide, 'there is nobody so happy as I shall be when I see Lady Cunégonde again.'

'There is no harm in hoping,' said Martin.

Days and weeks passed by, however; Cacambo did not return, and Candide was so depressed that he never even reflected that Pacquette and Brother Giroflée did not return to thank him.

CHAPTER XXVI

How Candide and Martin supped with six strangers, and who they were

ONE evening Candide and Martin were sitting down to table with some strangers who were staying in the same inn, when a man with a face the colour of soot came up and, taking Candide by the arm, said:

'Be ready to leave with us: do not fail.'

Candide turned, and recognised Cacambo. Only the sight of Cunégonde would have surprised and pleased him more. He was almost beside himself with joy, and embraced his old friend, saying:

'Surely Cunégonde is here, too. Where is she? Take me to her, so that she and I may die of joy together.'

'Cunégonde is not here,' said Cacambo, 'she is at Constantinople.'

'Constantinople?... Heavens alive!... However, if she were in China, I should fly to her. Let us go.'

'We shall leave after supper,' replied Cacambo; 'I can tell you no more; I am a slave, and my master is waiting for me; I must go and serve at table. Don't say a word. Eat your supper and be ready.'

Candide was distracted between joy and grief. Delighted as he was to see his faithful agent once more, he was astonished to see him a slave. Filled with the idea of finding his mistress again, he took his seat with beating heart and troubled mind. With him sat Martin, who had observed the incident with complete detachment, and six strangers who had come to Venice for the carnival.

Cacambo, who waited on one of the strangers, came up to his master when the meal was over and whispered in his ear:

'Sire, Your Majesty can leave when you wish. The gondola is ready.'

With these words he left the room. The astonished guests were looking at each other without saying a word, when another servant approached his master and said:

'Sire, Your Majesty's carriage is at Padua, and the boat is ready.'

His master nodded, and the servant went out. The remaining guests exchanged further glances, and showed increased surprise. A third valet then approached a third stranger, and said to him:

'Sire, if Your Majesty will take my advice, you will not stay here any longer: I will go and get everything ready for your departure.'

And he disappeared straight away.

Candide and Martin had no further doubt that these were characters in a masquerade taking part in the carnival. A fourth servant said to a fourth master,

'Your Majesty can leave when you wish,' and went out like the rest.

The fifth valet said as much to the fifth master. But the sixth valet spoke differently to the sixth stranger, who sat next to Candide. He said:

'Believe me, Sire, there's no more credit for Your Majesty or me. You and I will be in gaol to-night. I'm off to look after my own affairs. Good-bye.'

When all the servants had disappeared, Candide, Martin, and the six strangers maintained a profound silence. At last Candide broke it.

'Gentlemen,' said he, 'this is an unusual jest. How do you all come to be kings? For my part, I assure you that neither Martin nor I are anything of the sort.'

Cacambo's master replied gravely in Italian, and said:

'I am not jesting. My name is Achmet III. I was the Grand Sultan for several years. I dethroned my brother; then my nephew dethroned me, and had my viziers' throats cut; and now I have to drag out my days in the old seraglio. My nephew, the Grand Sultan Mahmoud, occasionally allows me to travel for my health, and I have come to Venice for the carnival.'

A young man who sat near Achmet spoke next. He said:

'My name is Ivan. I was once Emperor of all the Russias,

but was dethroned in my cradle. My father and mother were imprisoned, and I was brought up in captivity. I sometimes get leave to travel with my guards, and I have come to Venice for the carnival.'

The third said:

'I am Charles Edward, King of England. My father ceded me his sovereign rights, and I fought to maintain them. The hearts of eight hundred of my followers were torn out and used to beat their faces. I myself have been imprisoned. I am now on my way to Rome to visit my father, a dethroned monarch like my grandfather and myself, and I have come to Venice for the carnival.'

The fourth then took up the tale:

'I am the King of Poland,' he said; 'the fortune of war robbed me of my hereditary dominions, and my father suffered the same fate. I submit to Providence like Sultan Achmet, Emperor Ivan, and King Charles Edward, whom God preserve, and I have come to Venice for the carnival.'

The fifth said:

'I, too, am King of Poland. I lost my kingdom twice, but Providence gave me another realm, in which I have done more good than all the kings of the Sarmatians were ever able to do on the banks of the Vistula. I also submit to Providence, and have come to Venice for the carnival.'

It was now the turn of the sixth monarch to speak.

'Gentlemen,' said he, 'I cannot claim such noble origin as you. Yet I was once a king like any other. I am Theodore, who was elected King of Corsica. I was called "Your Majesty", yet at present I am scarcely called "Sir". I have had my own coinage, and now I haven't a farthing to my name. I have had two Secretaries of State, and now I have scarcely a servant. I have sat upon a throne, and have spent many weary days in a London prison on a bed of straw. I am much afraid I shall receive the same treatment here, though I have come to Venice like your Majesties for the carnival.'

The five other kings heard this story with gracious compassion. Each of them gave twenty sequins to King Theodore to buy clothes and shirts. Candide, however, presented him with a diamond worth two thousand sequins. 'Who is this mere commoner,' said the five kings, 'who is in a position to give a hundred times as much as each of us and who actually gives it?'

As they rose from table, there arrived at the same inn four Serene Highnesses who had also lost their estates by the fortunes of war and come to Venice for the remainder of the carnival. But Candide took no notice of these newcomers; his sole concern was to go to Constantinople to find his beloved Cunégonde.

CHAPTER XXVII

Candide's journey to Constantinople

THANKS to the faithful Cacambo, the Turkish captain who was to bring Sultan Achmet back to Constantinople agreed to take Candide and Martin on board, and they both embarked after paying their humble respects to His miserable Highness. As they made their way to the quayside, Candide said to Martin:

'To think that we have had supper with six dethroned kings, and, what is more, that amongst those six I have given charity to one! Perhaps there are many other princes even more unfortunate. For my part, I have lost nothing more than a hundred sheep, and I am hurrying to the arms of my Cunégonde. I have been thinking it over again, my dear Martin, and find that Pangloss was quite right; all is for the best.'

'I hope so,' said Martin.

'Was there ever a more unlikely adventure than ours at Venice?' said Candide. 'Six dethroned kings having supper together at an inn was a sight never seen or heard of before.'

'Surely no more unusual than most things that have happened to us,' said Martin. 'It is very common for kings to be dethroned; and as for the honour of having supper with them, it is a trifle which does not deserve our attention.'

Scarcely had Candide climbed on board when he drew his friend, Cacambo, on one side and said to his old servant:

'Tell me, how is Cunégonde? Is she still a prodigy of beauty? Does she love me still? How is she getting on? I suppose you have bought her a palace at Constantinople?'

'My dear master,' replied Cacambo, 'Cunégonde is washing dishes on the shores of the sea of Marmora for a monarch who has very few dishes to be washed. She is a slave in the house of an old Prince, called Ragotski, to whom the Grand Turk allows seven and sixpence a day as a refugee; but what is sadder still is that she has lost her beauty and has become horribly ugly.'

'Well, well,' said Candide, with a sigh. 'Beautiful or

ugly, I am an honest man, and my duty is to love her always. But how can she have been reduced to such a state with the five or six million you had about you?'

Cacambo showed impatience.

'Didn't I have to give two millions,' he said, 'to Don Fernando d'Ibaraa y Figueora y Mascarenes y Lampourdos y Souza, the Governor of Buenos Ayres, for permission to take Lady Cunégonde away? And didn't a brave pirate rob us of all the rest? And didn't this pirate take us to Cape Matapan, Melos, Nicaria, Samos, Patras, the Dardanelles, Marmora, and Scutari? Cunégonde and the old woman wait upon the Prince I mentioned, and I am the dethroned Sultan's slave.'

'What terrible calamities,' said Candide, 'and each dependent on another! But, after all, I have still a few diamonds left, so I shall easily deliver Cunégonde. It is a pity she has become so ugly, though.'

Turning to Martin, he continued:

'Who do you think has the most to complain of? Emperor Achmet, Emperor Ivan, King Charles Edward, or I?'

'I couldn't say,' replied Martin; 'I should have to look into your hearts to find out.'

'Now, if Pangloss were here,' said Candide, 'he would know and would tell us.'

'I don't know,' said Martin, 'what scales that Pangloss of yours could use to weigh the misfortunes of men and estimate their sorrows. All I can guess is that there are millions of men on the earth with a hundred times more to complain of than King Charles Edward, Emperor Ivan, and Sultan Achmet.'

'Very possibly,' said Candide.

After a few days they reached the Bosporus. The first thing Candide did was to buy Cacambo his freedom at a great price; and then, without loss of time, he set off in a boat with his companions for the shore of the Sea of Marmora to look for Cunégonde, however ugly she might be.

Amongst the galley-slaves there were two who rowed atrociously and were whipped from time to time on their naked shoulders by the Levantine captain. It was natural for Candide to regard them more closely than the other galley-slaves and to approach them with a look of pity. Disfigured as their faces were, certain features reminded him a little of Pangloss and that unfortunate Jesuit, the Baron, Cunégonde's brother. The mere resemblance stirred and troubled him, and he looked at them even more closely.

'I assure you,' said he to Cacambo, 'that if I hadn't seen Professor Pangloss hanged, and if I had not had the misfortune to kill the Baron, I should think that those two men rowing in this galley were they.'

On hearing the names of Pangloss and the Baron, the two galley-slaves uttered a great cry, stopped still at the bench, and allowed their oars to fall. The Levantine captain rushed at them and whipped them more furiously still.

'Stop, sir! Stop!' cried Candide. 'I will give you as much money as you want.'

'Good Heavens! It's Candide!' said one of the galley-slaves.

'Good Heavens! It's Candide!' said the other.

'Am I dreaming?' said Candide. 'Am I awake? Am I in this galley? Is that the Baron I killed? Is that Professor Pangloss, whom I saw hanged?'

'The same! The same!' they replied.

'What! Is that the great philosopher?' said Martin.

'Now, Captain,' said Candide. 'How much money do you want for the ransom of Lord Thunder-ten-tronckh, one of the principal barons of the Empire, and Professor Pangloss, the most profound metaphysician in all Germany?'

'As you are a Christian cur,' replied the Levantine captain, 'and as these curs, these Christian galley-slaves, are barons and metaphysicians, men, I suppose, of high rank in their country, you shall give me fifty thousand sequins for them.'

'You shall have them, sir. Take me back to Constantinople as quick as lightning, and you shall be paid on the spot. But I was forgetting—take me first to Lady Cunégonde's.' But on hearing Candide's first offer, the Levantine captain had already turned his boat towards the town, and was making his slaves row faster than a bird can cleave the air.

Candide embraced Pangloss and the Baron again and again.

'But how was it I did not kill you, my dear Baron?' he asked. 'And, my dear Pangloss, how do you come to be alive after being hanged? And why are you both galley-slaves in Turkey?'

'Is it really true that my dear sister is in this country?' said the Baron.

'Yes,' replied Cacambo.

'I behold my dear Candide once more!' cried Pangloss.

Candide introduced them to Martin and Cacambo. They embraced each other and began talking all at once. The galley made such good speed that they were soon back in port. A Jew was found to whom Candide sold for fifty thousand sequins a diamond worth a hundred thousand, the Jew swearing by Abraham that he could not offer more. Candide immediately paid ransom for the Baron and Pangloss. Pangloss threw himself at his liberator's feet and bathed them with his tears. The Baron, however, thanked him with a nod of his head and promised to pay him back the money at the first opportunity.

'But is it possible for my sister to be in Turkey?' said he.

'Nothing is more likely,' replied Cacambo, 'since she's washing dishes for a Prince of Transylvania.'

Two Jews were then produced, to whom Candide sold some more diamonds. Then they all set off in another galley to deliver Lady Cunégonde.

CHAPTER XXVIII

What happened to Candide, Cunégonde, Pangloss, Martin, and the rest

'FORGIVE me once more,' said Candide to the Baron; 'forgive me, Reverend Father, for striking you with a sword.'

'We will say no more about it,' said the Baron; 'I was a little too hasty, I admit. But since you want to know how you came to see me in the galleys, I must tell you that after I had been cured of my wound by the brother apothecary of the college, I was attacked and captured by a detachment of Spaniards and imprisoned at Buenos Ayres very soon after my sister had left. I asked to be sent back to Rome to the Father General of my order, and was later appointed chaplain to the French ambassador at Constantinople. It was scarcely a week after I had taken up my duties that one evening I met a handsome young lad who was one of the Sultan's pages. It was very hot, and the young man wanted to bathe, so I took the opportunity of bathing too. I did not know that it was a capital offence for a Christian to be found naked with a young Mussulman. A Turkish judge ordered me one hundred lashes on the soles of my feet and condemned me to the galleys. I do not think a more horrible piece of injustice was ever committed. But I should very much like to know why my sister is working in the kitchen of a Transylvanian sovereign who has taken refuge with the Turks.'

'Pangloss, my dear Pangloss,' said Candide, 'I never expected to see you again.'

'It is true,' said Pangloss, 'that you saw me hanged, though of course I ought to have been burnt. But you remember that it was pouring with rain when I was to be roasted. The storm was so violent that they gave up hope of lighting the fire, and I was hanged instead, as there was no better alternative. My body was bought by a surgeon, who carried me home to be dissected. He first of all made a crucial incision from the collar-bone to the navel. Now, no one could have been hanged more incompetently than I was. The chief executioner of the Holy Inquisition was a subdeacon, and a genius at burning people, but he was not accustomed to hanging. The rope was wet and failed to slide properly; it was knotted; so I was still breathing when they took me down. The crucial incision made me yell so loud that the surgeon recoiled; he must have thought he was dissecting the devil, for he rushed off in terror of his life, and fell down the staircase in his hurry. Hearing the noise, his wife ran in from a neighbouring room and saw me stretched out on the table with my crucial incision. She was even more terrified than her husband, and fell over his body as she fled. When they had picked themselves up, I heard the surgeon's wife say to the surgeon, "Whatever made you dissect a heretic, my dear? Don't you know that those folk are always possessed of the devil? I will go as quick as I can and fetch a priest to exorcise him." I trembled at her words, and recovered what strength was left me to cry for pity. At last this Portuguese barber took his courage in both hands and sewed up my skin, and even his wife was induced to look after me; so I was on my feet again at the end of a fortnight. The barber found me a place as footman to a Maltese knight who was going to Venice; but as my master had nothing to pay me with, I left him for a Venetian business man, whom I followed to Constantinople.

'One day I happened to enter a mosque, and found no one there but an old priest and a pretty young girl saying her prayers. Her dress was open at the neck, and between her breasts she had a beautiful bunch of tulips, roses, anemones, ranunculus, hyacinths, and auriculas. She dropped her bouquet, and I eagerly picked it up and reverently replaced it. But I took so long in adjusting it, that the priest flew into a rage, and, seeing that I was a Christian, called for help. I was taken before a judge, who ordered me a hundred lashes on the soles of my feet and sent me to the galleys. There I was chained in the very same galley and to the very same bench as the Baron. In that galley there were four young fellows from Marseilles, five Neapolitan priests, and two monks from Corfu, who told us that similar adventures happened every day. The Baron maintained that he had suffered a much greater injustice than I had, and I maintained that there is far less harm in replacing a bouquet on a woman's breast than in being found naked with the Sultan's page. We used to argue incessantly and to receive twenty lashes a day, until the sequence of events ordained in this universe brought you to our galley to ransom us.'

'Now, my dear Pangloss,' said Candide, 'tell me this. When you had been hanged, dissected, and beaten unmercifully, and while you were rowing at your bench, did you still think that everything in this world is for the best?'

'I still hold my original views,' replied Pangloss, 'for I am still a philosopher. It would not be proper for me to recant, especially as Leibnitz cannot be wrong; and besides, the *pre-established harmony*, together with the *plenum* and the *materia subtilis*, is the most beautiful thing in the world.

CHAPTER XXIX

How Candide found Cunégonde and the old woman once more

CANDIDE, the Baron, Pangloss, Martin, and Cacambo had many adventures to tell. They discussed which events have been contingent in this world and which have not, and they argued about effects and causes, moral and physical evil, free will and necessity, and the consolations to be found in Turkish galleys. While they were thus occupied they reached the shore of the Propontis at the Prince of Transylvania's house, and the first objects which met their gaze were Cunégonde and the old woman hanging out napkins on a line to dry.

The Baron blenched at the sight. Even the fond lover himself drew back aghast at seeing how weatherbeaten his lovely Cunégonde had become, for her eyes were bloodshot, her throat was wizened, her cheeks were wrinkled, and her arms were red and scaly. But his manners were so delicate that he immediately recovered his composure and advanced to meet her. Cunégonde embraced Candide and her brother, and they embraced the old woman. Candide then ransomed them both.

In the neighbourhood there was a small farm which the old woman suggested that Candide should take, while waiting for the party's fortunes to improve. Cunégonde did not know she had grown so ugly, since no one had told her; but as she now reminded Candide of his promises with the utmost firmness, the good man did not dare to refuse her. He then informed the Baron that he was going to marry his sister.

'I shall never allow her to disgrace herself so meanly,' said the Baron, 'and I shall not permit such insolence from you. With that disgrace at least I shall never be reproached. My sister's children could never enter the highest ranks of German society. No, my sister shall marry none but a baron of the Holy Roman Empire.'

Cunégonde threw herself at his feet and bathed them with her tears, but the Baron was inflexible.

'You unspeakable ass!' exclaimed Candide. 'I have taken you from the galleys and paid your ransom, and I have paid your sister's, too. I found her washing dishes, and she's as ugly as a witch. Yet when I have the decency to make her my wife, you still pretend to raise objections. I should kill you again, if my anger got the better of me.'

'You can kill me again, if you like,' said the Baron, 'but while I live, you shall never marry my sister.'

CHAPTER XXX

Conclusion

AT the bottom of his heart, Candide had no wish to marry Cunégonde, but the Baron's intransigence determined him to go through with the match; and besides, Cunégonde was pressing him so strongly that he could not retract. He consulted Pangloss, Martin, and the faithful Cacambo. Pangloss compiled a beautiful memorandum in which he proved that the Baron had no rights over his sister, and that in accordance with Imperial law she could give Candide her left hand in marriage. Martin recommended throwing the Baron into the sea, while Cacambo decided that he must be given back to the Levantine captain and replaced in the galleys, after which he should be sent to Rome to the Father General by the very first ship. Cacambo's advice seemed the most sensible, and was approved by the old woman, but nothing was said to Cunégonde about the plan. It was carried out at little cost, and they enjoyed the double pleasure of overreaching a Jesuit and punishing the pride of a German baron.

It would be natural to suppose that, after so many disasters, Candide should lead the most pleasing life imaginable, married at last to his mistress, and living with the philosophical Pangloss, the philosophical Martin, the prudent Cacambo, and the old woman, especially as he had brought away so many diamonds from the country once occupied by the Incas. But he had been so badly cheated by the Jews, that he had nothing left beyond his little farm. His wife daily grew uglier, and became more and more cantankerous and insufferable. The old woman was now quite infirm, and had developed an even worse temper than Cunégonde's. Cacambo, whose job was to work in the garden and sell vegetables in Constantinople, was quite worn out with toil, and cursed his lot. Pangloss was vexed to think that he was not the master spirit in some German university. As for Martin, he was firmly persuaded that a man is badly off wherever he is, so he suffered in patience. Candide, Martin, and Pangloss sometimes discussed metaphysics and morals. From the windows of the farmhouse boats were often seen passing, crowded with Turkish statesmen, military governors, and judges, bound for exile in Lemnos, Mytilene, or Erzerum, and other judges, governors, and statesmen were seen coming to take the place of the banished, only to be banished in their turn. Heads, too, were to be seen, decently empaled for display at the Sublime Porte. Sights such as these made the philosophers renew their disputations; and when there was no discussion, the boredom was so intolerable that the old woman was provoked one day to remark:

'I should like to know which is the worst, to be ravished a hundred times by negro pirates, to have one buttock cut off, to run the gauntlet of a Bulgar regiment, to be whipped and hanged at an auto-da-fé, to be dissected, to row in the galleys—in fact, to experience all the miseries through which we have passed—or just to stay here with nothing to do?'

'That's a difficult question,' said Candide.

The old woman's speech produced fresh reflections. Martin's conclusion was that man was born to suffer from the restlessness of anxiety or from the lethargy of boredom. Candide did not agree, but he admitted nothing. Pangloss allowed that his sufferings had been uniformly horrible; but as he had once maintained that everything would turn out right in some marvellous way, he still maintained it would, however little he believed it.

One day an incident occurred which confirmed Martin in his detestable views, and at the same time embarrassed Pangloss and made Candide more dubious than ever. It was the arrival of Pacquette and Brother Giroflée at the little farm in the utmost distress. They had soon got through their three thousand piastres, and had parted company only to be reconciled and to quarrel once again. They had been in prison and had escaped, and Brother Giroflée had at last turned Turk. Pacquette had continued to practise her profession but without a shadow of profit to herself.

'I knew quite well,' said Martin to Candide, 'that your presents would soon be spent and would leave them much worse off than before. You've squandered millions of piastres, you and Cacambo between you, and you are no happier than Brother Giroflée and Pacquette.'

'My dear child,' cried Pangloss to Pacquette, 'so Heaven has brought you back to us at last! Do you realise that you cost me an eye, an ear, and the end of my nose? What a state you are in! What a world this is!'

This fresh adventure drove them back to their discussions with redoubled ardour.

There lived in the neighbourhood a famous dervish, who was reputed to be the greatest philosopher in Turkey. They went to consult him, and chose Pangloss as their spokesman.

'Master,' said he, 'we have come to ask a favour. Will you kindly tell us why such a strange animal as man was ever made?'

'What has that got to do with you?' said the dervish. 'Is it your business?'

'But surely, reverend father,' said Candide, 'there is a great deal of evil in the world.'

'And what if there is?' said the dervish. 'When His Highness sends a ship to Egypt, do you suppose he worries whether the ship's mice are comfortable or not?'

'What ought to be done, then?' said Pangloss.

'Keep your mouth shut!' said the dervish.

'I had been looking forward,' said Pangloss, 'to a little discussion with you about cause and effect, the best of all possible worlds, the origin of evil, the nature of the soul, and pre-established harmony.'

At these words the dervish got up and slammed the door in their faces.

During this conversation, news had spread that two cabinet ministers and a judge had been strangled at Constantinople, and that several of their friends had been impaled. This catastrophe kept people talking for several hours. On their way back to the little farm, Pangloss, Candide, and Martin noticed an old man of patriarchal appearance sitting at his door under an arbour of orange-trees enjoying the fresh air. Pangloss, who liked gossip as much as argument, asked the old fellow the name of the judge who had been strangled.

'I have no idea,' he replied. 'I could not tell you the name of any judge or any minister. I am utterly ignorant of what you have been talking about. I suppose it's true that those who enter politics sometimes come to a miserable end, and deserve it; but I never bother myself about what happens in Constantinople. I send my garden stuff to be sold there, and that's enough for me.'

With these words, he invited the strangers into his house, where his two sons and daughters offered them several kinds of sherbet which they had made themselves, as well as drinks flavoured with candied lemon peel, oranges, lemons, citrons, pineapples, and pistachios, and pure Mocha coffee unmixed with the bad coffee you get from Batavia and the West Indies. After this refreshment the worthy Mussulman's two daughters perfumed the beards of the three visitors.

'You must have a magnificent estate,' said Candide to the Turk.

'Only twenty acres,' replied the Turk; 'my children help me to farm it, and we find that the work banishes those three great evils, boredom, vice, and poverty.'

As he walked back to the farm, Candide reflected on what the Turk had said. 'That old fellow,' said he, turning to Pangloss and Martin, 'seemed to me to have done much better for himself than those six kings we had the honour of supping with.'

'High estate,' said Pangloss, 'is always dangerous, as every philosopher knows. For Eglon, King of Moab, was assassinated by Ehud, and Absalom was hanged by his hair and stabbed with three spears; King Nadab, the son of Jeroboam, was killed by Baasha; King Elah by Zimri; Joram by Jehu; Athaliah by Jehoiada; and King Jehoiakim, King Jehoiachin, and King Zedekiah all became slaves. You know the miserable fate of Croesus, Astyages, Darius, Dionysius of Syracuse, Pyrrhus, Perseus, Hannibal, Jugurtha, Ariovistus, Caesar, Pompey, Nero, Otho, Vitellius, Domitian, Richard II of England, Edward II, Henry VI, Richard III, Mary Queen of Scots, Charles I, the three Henrys of France, and the Emperor Henry IV? You know . . .?'

'I also know,' said Candide, 'that we must go and work in the garden.'

'You are quite right,' said Pangloss. 'When man was placed in the Garden of Eden, he was put there "to dress it and to keep it", to work, in fact; which proves that man was not born to an easy life.'

'We must work without arguing,' said Martin; 'that is the only way to make life bearable.'

The entire household agreed to this admirable plan, and each began to exercise his talents. Small as the estate was, it bore heavy crops. There was no denying that Cunégonde was decidedly ugly, but she soon made excellent pastry. Pacquette was clever at embroidery, and the old woman took care of the linen. No one refused to work, not even Brother Giroflée, who was a good carpenter, and thus became an honest man. From time to time Pangloss would say to Candide:

'There is a chain of events in this best of all possible worlds; for if you had not been turned out of a beautiful mansion at the point of a jackboot for the love of Lady Cunégonde, and if you had not been involved in the Inquisition, and had not wandered over America on foot, and had not struck the Baron with your sword, and lost all those sheep you brought from Eldorado, you would not be here eating candied fruit and pistachio nuts.'

'That's true enough,' said Candide; 'but we must go and work in the garden.'